Stock Exchange for Dummies

STOCK EXCHANGE FOR DUMMIES

How Does a Company Benefit by Having Their Stock Listed On An Exchange?

By

John King

Stock Investing Expert

About Author

John King is a renowned expert in the field of stock exchange and financial markets. With a career spanning over two decades, he has become a trusted voice in understanding market dynamics and investment strategies. King's expertise encompasses various facets of stock trading, from technical analysis to market forecasting.

His insights have been featured in numerous financial publications and media outlets, where he offers advice and analysis on stock trends and market behavior. In addition to his media presence, King is a sought-after speaker at industry conferences and a consultant for financial institutions.

King's approach combines rigorous data analysis with a deep understanding of market psychology, helping investors and traders make informed decisions. His contributions to the field have established him as a leading authority in stock exchange practices and financial strategy.

Chapter 1: Understanding the Basics of Stock Investing

Section 1: Introduction to Stock Investing

Why Invest in Stocks?

Investing in stocks is one of the most popular ways for individuals to build wealth and achieve financial goals. Stocks represent ownership in a company, giving investors a stake in the business's success. By buying shares of a company, you become a part-owner and can benefit from the company's growth and profitability. This concept of ownership is at the core of why many people are drawn to stock investing.

One of the primary reasons to invest in stocks is the potential for high returns. Historically, the stock market has outperformed other types of investments, such as bonds, real estate, and savings accounts, over the long term. For instance, the average annual return of the S&P 500—a benchmark of the largest companies in the U.S.—has been about 10% over the past several decades. This rate of return, though not guaranteed, is significantly higher than what you'd typically earn from safer investments like government bonds or savings accounts, making stocks an attractive option for those looking to grow their wealth.

Stock investing also allows you to take advantage of the power of compounding. By reinvesting dividends and capital gains, your investment can grow exponentially over time. The longer you stay invested, the more time your money has to grow, thanks to the compounding effect. This makes stock investing particularly beneficial for long-term financial goals, such as retirement savings, funding a child's education, or building a nest egg for the future.

Additionally, investing in stocks provides you with the opportunity to be part of innovations and growth stories. Whether it's investing in tech giants like Apple and Microsoft, emerging green energy companies, or cutting-edge biotech firms, stock investing allows you to align your financial interests with industries and companies you believe in. This alignment can be financially rewarding and intellectually satisfying, as you watch your investments contribute to broader technological and societal advancements.

However, it's important to recognize that stock investing is not without risks. Stock prices can fluctuate widely due to market volatility, economic changes, or company-specific news. This inherent volatility means that, while stocks offer the potential for significant gains, they can also lead to losses, especially in the short term. Therefore, understanding both the benefits and risks of stock investing is crucial before diving into the market.

Benefits and Risks of Stock Investing

Benefits of Stock Investing:

1. **High Return Potential:**
   As mentioned earlier, stocks have historically provided higher returns than other asset classes over the long term. While individual stock performance can vary, the broader market trend has been upward, rewarding patient investors who hold onto their investments through market ups and downs.

2. **Dividend Income:**
   Many companies pay dividends to their shareholders, providing a regular income stream on top of potential capital gains. Dividends can be particularly appealing for those seeking passive income or looking to reinvest to accelerate portfolio growth. Dividends also offer some stability during market downturns, as they provide returns even when stock prices are down.

3. **Liquidity and Flexibility:**
   Stocks are generally highly liquid investments, meaning you can buy or sell them easily on a stock exchange with just a few clicks. This liquidity provides investors with

flexibility, allowing them to quickly react to market changes, sell holdings, or rebalance their portfolios as needed. This is in contrast to investments like real estate, which can take months or even years to sell.

4. **Ownership and Voting Rights:**
   When you buy stocks, you gain ownership in a company and often the right to vote on important company decisions, such as electing board members or approving major corporate policies. This ownership aspect connects investors to the companies they invest in, making them more engaged and informed about their investments.

5. **Protection Against Inflation:**
   Stocks have historically outperformed inflation over the long term, making them a good hedge against rising prices. As companies grow and increase their profits, their stock prices tend to rise, preserving your purchasing power even as the cost of goods and services increases.

6. **Diversification Opportunities:**
   The stock market offers a wide range of industries and sectors, from technology and healthcare to consumer goods and finance. This diversity allows investors to spread their investments across different companies and industries, reducing the risk associated with any single investment. Diversification helps balance out the performance of different investments, which can stabilize your portfolio over time.

Risks of Stock Investing:

1. **Market Volatility:**
   One of the most significant risks of stock investing is market volatility. Stock prices can swing dramatically due to various factors, including economic changes, geopolitical events, or shifts in investor sentiment. This volatility can lead to substantial losses, especially for those who need to sell their investments during a downturn.

2. **Loss of Capital:**
   Unlike bonds, which often guarantee some return of principal, investing in stocks comes with the risk of losing your initial investment. If a company performs poorly or goes bankrupt, its stock price can plummet, resulting in significant losses for shareholders. This risk underscores the importance of thorough research and diversification to mitigate the impact of any single underperforming stock.

3. **Emotional Decision-Making:**
   The stock market can be highly emotional, driven by fear and greed. Investors may be tempted to buy stocks during market highs due to fear of missing out or sell during lows due to panic, often leading to poor decision-making. This emotional roller coaster can result in buying high and selling low, which is the opposite of a successful investment strategy.

4. **Unpredictable External Factors:**
   Stock prices can be affected by factors beyond a

company's control, such as changes in interest rates, political instability, or natural disasters. These external events can cause sudden market swings that are difficult to predict and manage, adding an element of uncertainty to stock investing.

5. **Dividend Cuts or Suspensions:**
   While dividends are a great source of income, they are not guaranteed. Companies can cut or suspend dividend payments during financial hardship, impacting investors who rely on this income stream. This risk is particularly relevant during economic downturns when companies prioritize conserving cash over returning it to shareholders.

6. **Concentration Risk:**
   Investing heavily in a single stock or sector can expose you to significant risk if that investment performs poorly. Diversification can help mitigate this risk, but it requires careful planning and ongoing management of your portfolio to ensure a balanced approach.

Stock Investing vs. Other Investments

Investing in stocks is just one of many ways to grow your wealth. It's important to compare stock investing with other popular investment options to understand where it fits into your overall financial strategy.

1. Stocks vs. Bonds:

Bonds are debt instruments that pay investors a fixed interest rate over a specified period. Unlike stocks, which offer ownership in a company, bonds represent a loan made by the investor to the issuer (such as a corporation or government). Bonds are generally considered safer than stocks because they provide regular interest payments and return of principal upon maturity. However, they offer lower potential returns compared to stocks. While bonds can help stabilize a portfolio, they may not provide enough growth to keep pace with inflation, making them less suitable for long-term wealth building.

2. Stocks vs. Real Estate:
Real estate is another popular investment, often seen as a tangible and relatively stable asset. Real estate investments can generate income through rental payments and appreciate over time, offering a hedge against inflation. However, real estate requires significant upfront capital, ongoing maintenance, and can be illiquid, making it harder to sell quickly in times of need. Compared to stocks, real estate can be less volatile but also less flexible, as it's not as easy to diversify across multiple properties without significant capital.

3. Stocks vs. Savings Accounts and CDs:
Savings accounts and Certificates of Deposit (CDs) are safe, low-risk places to park your money, offering guaranteed returns in the form of interest. However, the returns on these investments are typically very low, often below the rate of inflation, meaning your purchasing power may erode over time. While these options are excellent for emergency funds or short-term savings, they are not suitable for long-term growth

compared to stocks, which offer higher returns despite their volatility.

4. Stocks vs. Mutual Funds and ETFs:
Mutual funds and Exchange-Traded Funds (ETFs) allow investors to pool their money and invest in a diversified portfolio of stocks, bonds, or other assets. These funds are managed by professionals and offer instant diversification, reducing the risk associated with individual stocks. While they provide a more hands-off approach to investing, mutual funds and ETFs still expose investors to market risk, albeit with lower volatility than investing directly in individual stocks. They are a great way for beginners to start investing in the stock market without the need for extensive research on specific companies.

5. Stocks vs. Commodities:
Commodities, such as gold, oil, and agricultural products, are another asset class that investors use for diversification and as a hedge against inflation. However, commodity prices can be highly volatile and influenced by factors such as weather, geopolitical tensions, and supply-demand imbalances. Unlike stocks, commodities do not generate income and are often seen as more speculative investments.

Comparing stock investing with other popular investment options helps illustrate where stocks fit into a broader financial strategy. Below is a table comparing stocks with bonds, real estate, and savings accounts.

Investment Type	Potential Return	Risk Level	Liquidity	Income Generation	Inflation Protection
Stocks	High (10% average)	High (volatile)	High (easily traded)	Dividends	High (long-term growth)
Bonds	Moderate (3-5%)	Low to Moderate	Moderate (depends on type)	Fixed interest payments	Low to Moderate
Real Estate	Moderate (6-8%)	Moderate	Low (illiquid)	Rental income	Moderate (property values)
Savings Accounts	Low (0.5-2%)	Very Low (safe)	Very High (immediate access)	Interest	Very Low

Key Points:

- **Stocks vs. Bonds**: Stocks offer higher return potential compared to bonds but come with higher volatility and risk. Bonds are safer and provide fixed interest payments, making them suitable for conservative investors or those seeking stable income. However, bonds may not keep pace with inflation, especially in a low-interest-rate environment.
- **Stocks vs. Real Estate**: Real estate investments can provide stable income through rental payments and capital appreciation over time. However, real estate is less liquid than stocks and requires significant upfront capital, maintenance, and management efforts. Stocks, on

the other hand, are easier to buy and sell, providing flexibility and diversification.

- **Stocks vs. Savings Accounts**: Savings accounts are incredibly safe but offer very low returns, often below inflation. They are best suited for emergency funds or short-term savings, not for long-term wealth growth. Stocks, despite their risks, provide a far better opportunity for long-term financial growth.

Investing in stocks offers a unique combination of high return potential, income generation, and ownership in some of the world's most successful companies. However, it also comes with risks, including market volatility and the potential for capital loss. Understanding these benefits and risks, as well as how stock investing compares to other investment options, is crucial for anyone considering entering the stock market. By aligning your investment choices with your financial goals, risk tolerance, and time horizon, you can make informed decisions that support your path to financial success.

Section 2: The History and Evolution of Stock Markets

The stock market has evolved over centuries, transforming from simple trading hubs into complex global financial systems that influence economies worldwide. Understanding the history of stock markets provides valuable insights into how they function today, the factors that drive market movements, and the lessons learned from past events. This section will explore the origins of stock markets, major historical events that have shaped their development, and the characteristics of the modern stock market landscape.

Origins of Stock Markets

The concept of trading shares and investing in companies dates back several centuries, with the first forms of stock markets emerging in Europe during the Renaissance period. The need for raising capital and sharing business risks drove the early development of financial markets, setting the foundation for the complex systems we see today.

1. **The Amsterdam Stock Exchange: The Birthplace of Modern Stock Trading**
   The world's first formal stock exchange was established in Amsterdam in 1602 by the Dutch East India Company (VOC). The VOC was the first company to issue stocks and bonds to the general public, allowing investors to buy shares in the company and participate in its profits. This innovation marked a significant shift in the way businesses were funded, as it allowed the VOC to raise substantial capital for its global trade operations while spreading financial risk among a large pool of investors.

   The Amsterdam Stock Exchange introduced key concepts that are still central to modern stock markets, including the trading of shares, dividends, and investor speculation. The exchange became a bustling center where traders, investors, and speculators gathered to buy and sell shares, making it the first organized marketplace for financial securities. The success of the Amsterdam

Stock Exchange set the stage for the creation of similar exchanges across Europe, laying the groundwork for the modern global financial system.

2. **The London Stock Exchange: Expansion of Financial Markets**
Following Amsterdam's lead, the London Stock Exchange (LSE) was officially established in 1801, although informal trading had been occurring in London's coffeehouses since the late 17th century. The LSE quickly grew to become one of the most important financial centers in the world, supporting Britain's expanding industrial economy and global trade network.

   The LSE played a crucial role in financing the Industrial Revolution, as companies sought capital to fund new technologies, infrastructure projects, and overseas ventures. The introduction of government regulations and standardized trading practices helped formalize the market, increasing investor confidence and expanding access to capital for a wide range of businesses.

3. **The New York Stock Exchange: The Rise of the U.S. Financial Powerhouse**
The New York Stock Exchange (NYSE) was officially founded in 1792 when 24 stockbrokers signed the Buttonwood Agreement under a buttonwood tree on Wall Street. This agreement established rules for trading securities and set the NYSE on a path to becoming the largest and most influential stock exchange in the world.

Throughout the 19th and early 20th centuries, the NYSE grew rapidly alongside the American economy, financing the expansion of railroads, industrial giants, and technological innovations. By the 1920s, the NYSE was the epicenter of global finance, symbolizing the dynamism of the U.S. economy and attracting investors from around the world. Today, the NYSE remains a dominant force in global finance, hosting many of the world's largest companies and playing a central role in shaping the modern stock market landscape.

Major Historical Events Affecting Stock Markets

The history of stock markets is marked by periods of exuberance and crisis, each leaving a lasting impact on how markets operate. Major historical events have shaped investor behavior, regulatory frameworks, and market structures, highlighting the inherent risks and opportunities of investing.

1. **The South Sea Bubble (1720): Early Lessons in Market Speculation**
   One of the earliest and most infamous financial bubbles was the South Sea Bubble of 1720. The South Sea Company, which was granted a monopoly on trade with South America by the British government, saw its stock price soar as investors speculated wildly on its future profits. The company's shares were heavily promoted and traded at inflated prices, driven by unrealistic expectations and rampant speculation.

When the bubble burst, many investors lost their fortunes, and the British government was forced to implement new regulations to restore public trust in the markets. The South Sea Bubble served as a stark reminder of the dangers of speculative mania and the need for transparency and oversight in financial markets.

2. **The Wall Street Crash of 1929 and the Great Depression**
   The stock market crash of 1929, which marked the beginning of the Great Depression, was one of the most devastating financial events in history. A period of speculative excess in the 1920s, fueled by easy credit and high investor confidence, led to unsustainable stock prices. When the market finally collapsed in October 1929, billions of dollars were wiped out, leading to widespread bank failures, mass unemployment, and a severe economic downturn.

   The crash exposed significant weaknesses in the financial system, including lack of regulation, excessive leverage, and inadequate investor protections. In response, the U.S. government introduced sweeping reforms, including the establishment of the Securities and Exchange Commission (SEC) in 1934, to regulate the stock market and restore investor confidence. The lessons learned from the 1929 crash continue to influence financial regulations today, underscoring the importance of market oversight and investor protection.

3. **The Dot-Com Bubble (1997-2000): The Rise and Fall of Technology Stocks**
   The late 1990s witnessed a boom in technology stocks driven by the rapid growth of the internet and speculation about the future potential of tech companies. Investors poured money into internet-based startups, often valuing them based on potential rather than actual earnings. Companies with little to no revenue saw their stock prices skyrocket, creating a speculative bubble.

   When the bubble burst in 2000, many tech companies collapsed, and investors lost billions. The dot-com crash underscored the risks of investing in overvalued stocks and highlighted the importance of fundamental analysis and realistic expectations. Despite the crash, the internet revolution eventually proved transformative, and many surviving tech companies, like Amazon and Google, went on to become dominant players in the global economy.

4. **The 2008 Financial Crisis: Global Market Collapse and Recovery**
   The 2008 financial crisis was triggered by the collapse of the U.S. housing market and the subsequent failure of major financial institutions. Excessive risk-taking, poor lending practices, and complex financial derivatives led to a global market meltdown, resulting in severe economic consequences worldwide. Stock markets plunged, millions lost their jobs, and governments were

forced to implement massive bailouts to stabilize the financial system.

In the aftermath, stricter regulations were introduced to prevent future crises, including the Dodd-Frank Act in the U.S., which aimed to increase transparency and reduce systemic risks in the financial sector. The crisis highlighted the interconnectedness of global markets and the importance of robust regulatory frameworks to maintain financial stability.

The Modern Stock Market Landscape

Today's stock market is a highly sophisticated and interconnected global system, influenced by technological advancements, regulatory changes, and evolving investor behavior. Modern stock markets are characterized by increased accessibility, high-speed trading, and a broad range of investment options.

1. **Globalization and the Rise of International Markets** Modern stock markets are no longer confined to national borders. Exchanges such as the Tokyo Stock Exchange, London Stock Exchange, and Hong Kong Stock Exchange have become major players, attracting companies and investors from around the world. The growth of international markets has provided investors with access to a wider range of investment opportunities, allowing them to diversify their portfolios across different regions and sectors.

The rise of emerging markets, such as China and India, has further expanded the global stock market landscape. These markets offer high growth potential but also come with increased volatility and political risk, requiring investors to carefully consider their exposure to different regions.

2. **Technological Advancements: High-Frequency Trading and Digital Platforms**
   Technological innovations have revolutionized how stock markets operate, making trading faster, cheaper, and more accessible. High-frequency trading (HFT), which uses algorithms to execute trades in milliseconds, has significantly increased market liquidity but also introduced new challenges, such as market manipulation and flash crashes.

   The rise of online trading platforms and mobile apps has democratized access to the stock market, allowing individual investors to buy and sell stocks with ease. This accessibility has led to the growth of retail investing, where individuals participate directly in the market rather than through traditional financial advisors.

3. **ETFs and Index Funds: New Tools for Diversification and Passive Investing**
   Exchange-Traded Funds (ETFs) and index funds have become popular investment vehicles, offering investors an easy way to diversify their portfolios and gain exposure to broad market indices. ETFs trade like stocks

on exchanges and provide a cost-effective way to invest in a wide range of assets, from large-cap stocks to niche sectors like technology, healthcare, or commodities.

The growth of passive investing, where funds aim to replicate the performance of a market index rather than actively selecting individual stocks, has reshaped the investment landscape. Passive strategies offer lower fees and have often outperformed active managers, making them an attractive option for many investors.

4. **Regulation and Investor Protection: Safeguarding Market Integrity**
   Modern stock markets are heavily regulated to ensure transparency, fairness, and investor protection. Regulatory bodies such as the SEC in the U.S., the Financial Conduct Authority (FCA) in the UK, and the European Securities and Markets Authority (ESMA) oversee market activities, enforce rules, and protect investors from fraud and market abuse.

   Enhanced regulations, including stricter disclosure requirements and improved market surveillance, have helped maintain trust in the financial system. However, challenges remain, such as navigating the regulatory implications of new technologies like cryptocurrencies and blockchain.

The history and evolution of stock markets illustrate the dynamic nature of financial markets and the complex interplay of innovation, speculation, regulation, and global economic forces. From the early days of the Amsterdam Stock Exchange to the high-tech trading floors of today, stock markets have continually adapted to changing economic landscapes, investor behavior, and technological advancements.

Major historical events, such as market bubbles, crashes, and financial crises, serve as important lessons in the importance of market regulation, investor education, and the need for balanced, informed investing. The modern stock market landscape, shaped by globalization, technological innovation, and evolving investment strategies, offers unprecedented opportunities for wealth creation but also requires a careful understanding of the risks involved.

As investors, understanding the history of stock markets helps us navigate the complexities of today's financial environment and make better decisions to achieve our long-term financial goals.

Section 3: Why Stocks Matter to the Economy

The stock market plays a vital role in the functioning of the global economy. It acts as a powerful engine for economic growth, influences businesses and individuals, and serves as a barometer for overall economic health. This section delves into the importance of stocks in the economy, examining their impact on economic growth, their influence on businesses and individuals, and their role as a key economic indicator.

The Role of Stocks in Economic Growth

Stocks are not just financial instruments; they are the lifeblood of economic growth and development. The stock market provides a platform where companies can raise capital by issuing shares to the public, enabling them to fund expansion, innovation, and other business activities. Here's how stocks contribute to economic growth:

1. **Raising Capital for Business Expansion**
   One of the primary functions of the stock market is to enable companies to raise capital. When a company goes public through an initial public offering (IPO), it issues shares to investors in exchange for capital. This influx of funds allows businesses to invest in new projects, expand operations, develop new products, and enter new markets. The ability to access capital through the stock market is particularly crucial for startups and high-growth companies that need substantial funds to scale.

   For instance, tech giants like Apple, Google, and Amazon raised billions of dollars through the stock market, which allowed them to invest heavily in research and development, leading to groundbreaking innovations. This, in turn, spurs productivity, creates jobs, and drives economic growth.

2. **Facilitating Efficient Capital Allocation**
   The stock market plays a critical role in the efficient allocation of resources within the economy. By providing a transparent and regulated marketplace, the stock market

helps channel funds from savers (investors) to businesses that need capital for growth. This process ensures that money is directed towards companies with the best growth prospects, contributing to a more productive and dynamic economy.

Investors, through buying and selling shares, effectively vote on the future prospects of companies, rewarding those that demonstrate strong financial performance and innovative capabilities. This market-driven allocation of resources helps ensure that capital is used most effectively, supporting industries and companies that drive economic progress.

3. **Wealth Creation and Consumer Spending**
The stock market also contributes to economic growth by creating wealth for individuals and households. When stock prices rise, the value of investments in retirement accounts, mutual funds, and other equity-based assets increases, boosting the overall wealth of investors. This wealth effect can lead to increased consumer confidence and higher spending, which drives demand for goods and services in the economy.

For example, during bull markets (periods of rising stock prices), investors often feel more financially secure and are more likely to make significant purchases, such as homes, cars, and other consumer goods. This increased spending fuels economic activity and helps sustain growth. Conversely, during bear markets (periods of declining stock prices), reduced wealth can lead to lower consumer spending, highlighting the stock market's influence on economic cycles.

4. **Supporting Innovation and Entrepreneurship**
   The stock market provides a crucial avenue for funding innovative companies and new technologies. Many of the world's most transformative companies, particularly in technology, biotechnology, and renewable energy, rely on stock market funding to bring their ideas to life. By investing in these companies, the public helps drive technological advancements that enhance productivity, improve quality of life, and create new industries.

   The stock market's role in funding innovation is evident in sectors such as electric vehicles, artificial intelligence, and healthcare, where significant investment is required for research, development, and commercialization. By supporting innovation, the stock market helps foster long-term economic growth and competitiveness.

How Stocks Influence Businesses and Individuals

The influence of stocks extends beyond companies and investors to impact the broader economy. Stocks affect business decisions, individual financial planning, and overall economic stability.

1. **Impact on Corporate Decision-Making**
   Publicly traded companies are constantly under the scrutiny of investors, analysts, and regulators, which

influences their strategic decisions. Stock prices reflect market perceptions of a company's future performance, and management teams are often incentivized to focus on maximizing shareholder value. This dynamic can drive companies to make decisions that enhance profitability, such as cost-cutting measures, investments in new technologies, or entering new markets.

However, the pressure to meet short-term earnings expectations can also lead to challenges. Companies may prioritize immediate stock price gains over long-term growth initiatives, potentially cutting back on research and development or deferring necessary investments. This balance between short-term performance and long-term strategy is a critical consideration for companies influenced by their stock market performance.

2. **Influence on Individual Financial Planning and Retirement**
   Stocks are a cornerstone of personal financial planning, playing a vital role in wealth accumulation, retirement savings, and income generation. Many individuals invest in stocks directly or indirectly through retirement accounts, such as 401(k)s and IRAs, or through mutual funds and exchange-traded funds (ETFs). Over time, stocks have historically provided higher returns compared to other asset classes, making them an essential component of long-term investment strategies.

For retirees, dividends from stocks can provide a valuable source of income, helping to supplement pensions or social security. The performance of the stock market directly affects the financial well-being of millions of individuals, influencing their ability to fund education, buy homes, and achieve financial independence.

However, the volatility of stocks also presents risks, particularly for those nearing retirement who may be more exposed to market downturns. This underscores the importance of diversification and risk management in personal financial planning.

3. **Creation of Job Opportunities**
Companies that access capital through the stock market often use the funds to hire new employees, expand their operations, and enter new markets. This job creation is a direct result of the company's ability to grow and invest, fueled by stock market investment. For example, when a company expands its manufacturing facilities, it not only creates jobs within the company but also generates employment opportunities in related sectors such as construction, logistics, and supply chain management.

Moreover, the financial services industry, including stockbrokers, analysts, fund managers, and investment advisors, relies heavily on the stock market. The jobs created within this industry support economic growth by providing essential services that facilitate market transactions and help investors make informed decisions.

4. **Enhancing Access to Investment Opportunities** The stock market democratizes access to investment opportunities, allowing individuals to invest in a broad range of companies across different sectors and geographies. This accessibility enables people to participate in economic growth by owning a share of successful companies, regardless of their level of wealth. Through fractional shares, mutual funds, and ETFs, even small investors can diversify their portfolios and benefit from the potential upside of the market.

   Additionally, the stock market provides liquidity, allowing investors to buy and sell shares relatively quickly. This liquidity offers flexibility in financial planning, as individuals can adjust their investments in response to changing market conditions, personal needs, or economic outlooks.

The Stock Market as an Economic Indicator

The stock market is often referred to as a leading economic indicator, providing valuable insights into the overall health of the economy. Movements in stock prices reflect investor sentiment, expectations for corporate earnings, and broader economic trends, making the market a barometer for economic performance.

1. **Stock Market Performance and Economic Outlook**
   The stock market's performance is closely watched by economists, policymakers, and investors as a gauge of future economic activity. Rising stock prices typically signal optimism about the economy, reflecting expectations of strong corporate earnings, low unemployment, and robust consumer spending. Conversely, declining stock prices can indicate concerns about economic downturns, reduced corporate profits, or potential financial crises.

   For instance, during periods of economic expansion, stock markets often experience bull runs as investors anticipate continued growth and higher corporate earnings. In contrast, during recessions or periods of economic uncertainty, stock markets tend to decline, reflecting reduced business confidence and lower expectations for future growth.

   The relationship between stock market performance and economic outlook is not always straightforward, as markets can be influenced by external factors such as geopolitical events, changes in monetary policy, or investor psychology. However, overall trends in stock prices remain a valuable tool for assessing the direction of the economy.

2. **Market Sentiment and Consumer Confidence**
   The stock market also plays a crucial role in shaping consumer confidence, which is a key driver of economic

activity. When stock prices are rising, individuals feel wealthier and more confident about their financial future, which can lead to increased spending on goods and services. This, in turn, boosts business revenues, supports job creation, and contributes to economic growth.

Conversely, a declining stock market can have the opposite effect, leading to reduced consumer confidence and spending. This "wealth effect" highlights the interconnectedness of the stock market and the broader economy, as changes in investor sentiment can ripple through to impact real economic activity.

3. **Signals for Monetary and Fiscal Policy**
   Policymakers often look to the stock market as an indicator when making decisions about monetary and fiscal policy. Central banks, such as the Federal Reserve, monitor stock market performance as part of their assessment of financial conditions. For example, a sharp decline in stock prices might prompt central banks to consider easing monetary policy, such as lowering interest rates or implementing quantitative easing, to support economic growth.

   Governments may also respond to stock market conditions with fiscal measures, such as stimulus packages or tax incentives, to boost consumer spending and business investment. The market's performance serves as a feedback mechanism, helping policymakers gauge the effectiveness of their actions and adjust strategies as needed.

4. **Predictive Power of Stock Market Indicators**
   Various stock market indicators, such as the yield curve, stock market indices, and sector performance, are used to predict future economic trends. For example, the yield curve, which plots the interest rates of bonds with different maturities, is often watched for signs of economic recession. An inverted yield curve, where short-term rates are higher than long-term rates, has historically been a reliable predictor of economic downturns.

   Similarly, stock market indices, such as the S&P 500 or Dow Jones Industrial Average, provide snapshots of the overall market and are closely correlated with broader economic performance. Sector performance within the stock market, such as strength in consumer discretionary stocks or weakness in industrials, can also provide insights into underlying economic trends.

Stocks are a cornerstone of the modern economy, playing a pivotal role in driving economic growth, influencing corporate and individual decision-making, and serving as a key indicator of economic health. By providing companies with access to capital, supporting job creation, and offering investment opportunities to the public, the stock market contributes significantly to economic development.

The stock market's influence extends beyond financial markets, impacting consumer confidence, guiding policy decisions, and reflecting broader economic trends. Understanding the role of stocks in the economy highlights their importance not only for investors but also for the overall functioning of the global economy. As such, the stock market remains a critical component of economic growth and stability, shaping the financial landscape for businesses, individuals, and nations alike.

Chapter 2: Defining Stocks and Ownership

Section 1: Definition and Basic Concepts

Understanding stocks is fundamental to grasping how financial markets operate and how investors engage with companies. Stocks are not merely pieces of paper or digital entries; they represent a share of ownership in a company, and come with specific rights and privileges. This section explores the essence of stocks, including how they symbolize company ownership, the different types of stocks available, and the associated ownership rights.

How Stocks Represent Company Ownership

Stocks are financial instruments that signify ownership in a company. When an individual buys shares of a company, they are essentially purchasing a stake in that business, becoming a partial owner. This ownership is reflected in the form of equity, which represents a claim on the company's assets and earnings. Here's how stocks encapsulate the concept of ownership:

1. **Equity Ownership**
   Owning stock in a company grants shareholders equity, meaning they hold a claim on the company's net assets and earnings. Equity ownership can be compared to owning a piece of a pie—each share represents a slice of the company. This ownership entitles shareholders to a portion of the company's profits, typically through dividends, and provides them with a stake in the company's value, which can increase or decrease with market fluctuations.

2. **Types of Shares**
   Companies issue different types of shares to raise capital and distribute ownership. The most common types of shares are common shares and preferred shares, each offering distinct rights and benefits:

   •

- **Common Shares:** These represent the most basic form of ownership. Holders of common shares have voting rights on corporate matters, such as electing the board of directors and approving major changes. They also have the potential to receive dividends, though these are not guaranteed. In the event of liquidation, common shareholders are last in line to receive any remaining assets after all debts and preferred shareholders have been paid.
- **Preferred Shares:** Preferred shares provide a higher claim on assets and earnings compared to common shares. Preferred shareholders typically receive dividends before common shareholders and have a fixed dividend rate. They usually do not have voting rights, but they have priority over common shareholders in the event of liquidation. Preferred shares may also include features such as convertibility into common shares or callable provisions allowing the company to repurchase them.

3. **Stock Issuance and Market Capitalization**
   Companies issue stocks through an initial public offering (IPO) to raise capital for growth and expansion. After the IPO, stocks are traded on stock exchanges, such as the New York Stock Exchange (NYSE) or NASDAQ. The total market value of a company's outstanding shares is referred to as its market capitalization, or market cap.

Market cap is calculated by multiplying the stock price by the number of outstanding shares, providing a measure of the company's total value.

- **Market Capitalization Categories:** Companies are often classified based on their market cap:
  - **Large Cap:** Companies with a market cap exceeding $10 billion, generally considered stable and established.
  - **Mid Cap:** Companies with a market cap between $2 billion and $10 billion, often in growth phases.
  - **Small Cap:** Companies with a market cap between $300 million and $2 billion, potentially higher growth but with greater risk.
  - **Micro Cap:** Companies with a market cap below $300 million, often more volatile and speculative.

Types of Stocks

Stocks come in various types, each offering different features and benefits to investors. Understanding these types helps investors make informed decisions based on their investment goals, risk tolerance, and financial needs.

1. **Common Stock**
   Common stock is the most prevalent type of equity investment. Holders of common stock have voting rights, which allows them to participate in important corporate

decisions, such as mergers and acquisitions or changes in corporate policies. Common shareholders may receive dividends, but these are not fixed and can vary based on the company's performance and board of directors' decisions. Common stockholders also benefit from capital appreciation—an increase in the stock's value over time.

- **Characteristics of Common Stock:**
    - **Voting Rights:** Common shareholders have the right to vote on corporate matters.
    - **Dividends:** Dividends are variable and not guaranteed.
    - **Capital Appreciation:** Potential for stock price increase.
    - **Risk:** Last in line to receive assets in liquidation.

2. **Preferred Stock**

   Preferred stockholders have a higher claim on assets and earnings than common stockholders. They typically receive fixed dividends, which are paid out before any dividends are distributed to common shareholders. Preferred stock often lacks voting rights but may offer other features, such as convertibility into common stock or callability by the issuing company.

- **Characteristics of Preferred Stock:**
    - **Fixed Dividends:** Dividends are generally fixed and paid before common dividends.

    - **Priority in Liquidation:** Higher claim on assets in the event of liquidation.
    - **Limited Voting Rights:** Generally no voting rights.
    - **Convertible:** May have the option to convert into common stock.

3. **Growth Stocks**

   Growth stocks represent shares in companies expected to grow at an above-average rate compared to other companies. These stocks typically do not pay dividends, as the companies reinvest profits to fund expansion and innovation. Investors buy growth stocks with the expectation of capital appreciation as the company's earnings and stock price increase.

   - **Characteristics of Growth Stocks:**
     - **High Growth Potential:** Expected to grow faster than the market average.
     - **No Dividends:** Profits are reinvested rather than paid out as dividends.
     - **Volatility:** Can be more volatile due to high growth expectations.

4. **Value Stocks**

   Value stocks are shares in companies that are considered undervalued based on fundamental analysis. These stocks often have lower price-to-earnings (P/E) ratios and may provide dividends. Investors buy value stocks with the expectation that the market will eventually recognize the company's true value, leading to capital appreciation.

- **Characteristics of Value Stocks:**
    - **Undervalued:** Trading below their intrinsic value based on financial metrics.
    - **Dividend Potential:** Often provide dividends.
    - **Stable:** Generally considered more stable compared to growth stocks.

5. **Dividend Stocks**
   Dividend stocks are shares in companies that pay regular dividends to shareholders. These stocks are attractive to income-focused investors who seek a steady stream of income in addition to potential capital appreciation. Dividend stocks are often found in established companies with stable earnings.

- **Characteristics of Dividend Stocks:**
    - **Regular Income:** Provides consistent dividend payments.
    - **Stable:** Typically in well-established companies.
    - **Income Focused:** Ideal for retirees or income-seeking investors.

6. **Blue-Chip Stocks**
   Blue-chip stocks are shares in large, well-established, and financially sound companies with a history of reliable performance. These companies often have a strong market presence, stable earnings, and a track record of paying dividends. Blue-chip stocks are

considered safe and are popular among conservative investors.

- **Characteristics of Blue-Chip Stocks:**
    - **Established Companies:** Large, reputable, and financially stable.
    - **Reliable Performance:** Consistent earnings and dividends.
    - **Lower Risk:** Generally considered lower risk compared to smaller companies.

Ownership and Shareholder Rights

Stock ownership comes with various rights and privileges that empower shareholders to influence corporate governance and benefit from the company's success. These rights can vary based on the type of stock held and the specific policies of the company.

1. **Voting Rights**
   Voting rights are a fundamental aspect of shareholder ownership. Common shareholders typically have the right to vote on key issues at annual general meetings (AGMs) or special meetings. Voting rights include electing the board of directors, approving major corporate actions, and deciding on matters such as stock splits or mergers. The ability to vote on these matters gives shareholders a voice in the direction and management of the company.

- **Direct Voting:** Shareholders can vote in person at meetings or by proxy.
- **Influence:** Voting power is proportional to the number of shares owned, giving larger shareholders more influence.

2. **Dividends and Profit-Sharing**
   Shareholders benefit from dividends, which are distributions of a company's profits. Dividends provide a return on investment and are typically paid on common shares, though preferred shares often receive fixed dividends. The amount and frequency of dividends are determined by the board of directors and depend on the company's profitability and financial health.

   - **Dividend Payments:** Common dividends vary and are not guaranteed, while preferred dividends are fixed and paid before common dividends.
   - **Reinvestment:** Dividends can be reinvested in additional shares or used as income.

3. **Rights in Liquidation**
   In the event of liquidation, shareholders have rights to the company's remaining assets after all debts and preferred shareholders have been paid. Common shareholders are last in line to receive any residual value, which means they may receive little to no compensation if the company is not profitable or has substantial liabilities.

   - **Order of Claims:** Preferred shareholders have priority over common shareholders.

- **Residual Value:** Common shareholders receive any remaining assets after debts and preferred shares are settled.

4. **Information Rights**
Shareholders are entitled to receive information about the company's financial performance and governance. This includes annual reports, financial statements, and meeting minutes. Access to this information allows shareholders to make informed decisions about their investments and monitor the company's progress.

    - **Annual Reports:** Provides comprehensive details on financial performance and business operations.
    - **Transparency:** Ensures shareholders are informed about significant developments and corporate actions.

5. **Legal Protections**
Shareholders have legal protections to safeguard their rights and interests. These protections include the right to bring derivative actions against directors for breaches of fiduciary duty, participate in class actions for company-wide issues, and challenge decisions that adversely affect their interests.

    - **Derivative Actions:** Legal actions brought by shareholders on behalf of the company.
    - **Class Actions:** Legal actions involving multiple shareholders seeking redress for common grievances.

Stocks are a powerful tool for representing ownership in a company and come with a range of rights and privileges. Understanding the basics of stock ownership, including the different types of stocks and their associated rights, is crucial for investors. From voting rights and dividends to legal protections and information access, stocks offer various ways for shareholders to engage with and benefit from their investments.

The types of stocks—common, preferred, growth, value, dividend, and blue-chip—each cater to different investment goals and risk profiles. By grasping these concepts, investors can make informed decisions, align their investments with their financial objectives, and actively participate in the corporate governance of the companies they invest in.

Section 2: Ownership and Shareholder Rights

Owning shares of stock represents owning a fraction of a company. This ownership entitles shareholders to various rights and benefits, though the extent and nature of these rights can vary based on the type of stock and the shareholder's position within the company. This section delves into the key aspects of ownership and shareholder rights, including voting rights, dividends, and the impact of being a minority shareholder.

Voting Rights and Shareholder Influence

One of the fundamental rights of shareholders is the ability to vote on important company matters. Voting rights are an essential aspect of shareholder influence and corporate governance, allowing investors to have a say in the direction and management of the company. Here's a closer look at how voting rights work and their implications for shareholders:

1. **Types of Voting Rights**
   Shareholders typically possess voting rights based on the type of shares they own. Common shareholders generally have the right to vote on a range of significant issues, including:

   - **Elections of the Board of Directors:** Shareholders elect the members of the board of directors, who are responsible for overseeing the company's management and making strategic decisions.
   - **Approval of Major Corporate Actions:** Major corporate decisions, such as mergers and acquisitions, changes to the company's charter, or issuance of new shares, often require shareholder approval.
   - **Executive Compensation Plans:** Shareholders may vote on proposals related to executive compensation, stock option plans, and other financial matters affecting management.

   Preferred shareholders, on the other hand, usually do not have voting rights. Their preference lies in receiving fixed dividends and having priority over common shareholders in the event of liquidation, but they forgo the ability to influence corporate decisions.

2. **Voting Mechanisms**
   Shareholders typically exercise their voting rights during the annual general meeting (AGM) or special meetings convened by the company. Voting can be done in person, by proxy, or electronically, depending on the company's policies and applicable regulations. A proxy is an appointed representative who votes on behalf of a shareholder who cannot attend the meeting in person.

   The voting process may involve simple majority votes or more complex requirements, such as supermajority votes for specific actions. For instance, approving a merger might require a two-thirds majority of the votes cast. The outcomes of these votes can significantly impact the company's direction and governance.

3. **Influence of Voting Rights**
   Voting rights provide shareholders with a mechanism to influence corporate governance and decision-making. Shareholders can affect company policies, strategic direction, and leadership choices through their votes. However, the influence of individual shareholders can vary based on the size of their ownership stake.

   Institutional investors, such as mutual funds and pension funds, often hold substantial shares and wield significant voting power. Their votes can shape corporate policies and drive shareholder proposals, such as environmental, social, and governance (ESG) initiatives. Individual shareholders with smaller stakes might have less influence but can still participate in the democratic process of corporate governance.

Dividends and Profit-Sharing

Dividends represent a portion of a company's profits distributed to shareholders. They are a key benefit of owning stock and serve as a form of profit-sharing between the company and its investors. Here's an overview of how dividends work and their implications for shareholders:

1. **Understanding Dividends**
   Dividends are typically paid on common shares, though preferred shares may also receive fixed dividends. Companies usually declare dividends on a quarterly or annual basis, with the amount and frequency determined by the board of directors. The dividend payment is expressed as a dollar amount per share or as a percentage of the stock's price, known as the dividend yield.

   - **Dividend Declaration:** The board of directors announces the dividend amount, record date, and payment date. The record date determines which shareholders are eligible to receive the dividend, while the payment date is when the dividend is distributed.
   - **Dividend Reinvestment:** Shareholders can choose to reinvest dividends into additional shares through a dividend reinvestment plan (DRIP), allowing for compounding growth over time.

2. **Impact on Shareholder Returns**
   Dividends provide shareholders with a steady income stream, contributing to their overall returns on investment. For income-focused investors, such as retirees or those seeking regular cash flow, dividends are a crucial component of their investment strategy. Companies that consistently pay and increase dividends are often viewed favorably, as they signal financial stability and shareholder commitment.

   However, not all companies pay dividends. Growth-oriented companies, particularly in technology or emerging industries, may reinvest their profits into research and development, acquisitions, or expansion rather than distributing them to shareholders. These companies might attract investors seeking capital appreciation rather than income.

3. **Dividend Policies and Impact**
   A company's dividend policy reflects its financial health and management's approach to profit distribution. Companies with a strong track record of paying and increasing dividends are often perceived as financially robust and reliable investments. Conversely, a reduction or suspension of dividends might signal financial trouble or a shift in company strategy, potentially affecting stock prices and investor sentiment.

   Dividends also have tax implications for shareholders, as dividend income is generally subject to taxation. The tax treatment of dividends can vary by jurisdiction and individual tax situation, influencing investor decisions and the attractiveness of dividend-paying stocks.

Impact of Being a Minority Shareholder

While owning shares entitles investors to certain rights, the experience and influence of minority shareholders can differ significantly from that of major shareholders. Minority shareholders hold a smaller proportion of the company's equity, which can impact their rights and influence. Here's a closer look at the implications of being a minority shareholder:

1. **Limited Voting Power**
   Minority shareholders, by definition, hold a smaller percentage of the company's shares compared to major shareholders or institutional investors. As a result, their voting power is limited, and they may have less influence over corporate decisions and governance. While they can participate in voting on key issues, their votes may carry less weight compared to those of larger shareholders.

   Despite this, minority shareholders still have the right to vote on significant matters and can collectively band together to exert influence. Shareholder advocacy groups and activist investors often work to represent the interests of minority shareholders and push for changes that align with their goals.

2. **Access to Information and Transparency**
   Minority shareholders are entitled to access certain

information about the company, such as annual reports, financial statements, and meeting minutes. However, they might have less direct access to detailed operational data or insider information compared to major shareholders.

Companies are required to provide regular disclosures and maintain transparency to ensure all shareholders are informed about the company's performance and strategic direction. This transparency helps minority shareholders make informed decisions and understand the potential impact of corporate actions on their investments.

3. **Legal Protections and Shareholder Rights**
Minority shareholders have legal rights and protections to safeguard their interests. These protections can include the right to challenge decisions that they believe are detrimental to their interests, seek redress for breaches of fiduciary duty by directors, and participate in shareholder class actions.

In some jurisdictions, laws and regulations provide additional protections for minority shareholders, such as appraisal rights, which allow them to demand fair compensation if they disagree with certain corporate actions, such as mergers or acquisitions. These legal avenues help ensure that minority shareholders are not unfairly disadvantaged or excluded from important decisions affecting their investments.

4. **Potential for Influence through Shareholder Proposals**
   Minority shareholders can also influence corporate governance through shareholder proposals. They can submit proposals for consideration at annual meetings, addressing issues such as executive compensation, environmental practices, or corporate social responsibility. While the success of these proposals depends on the level of support from other shareholders, they represent a mechanism for minority shareholders to voice their concerns and advocate for changes.

   Activist shareholders, who hold significant but not necessarily controlling stakes, often use shareholder proposals and public campaigns to push for changes in corporate strategy or management practices. Their efforts can draw attention to issues and generate support from other investors, potentially leading to meaningful changes.

Ownership of stocks comes with a range of rights and responsibilities that impact both the individual shareholder and the broader company. Voting rights enable shareholders to influence corporate governance and major decisions, while dividends provide a way to share in the company's profits. However, the experience of being a minority shareholder comes with its own set of challenges, including limited voting power and access to information.

Understanding these aspects of stock ownership helps investors navigate their roles and make informed decisions about their investments. Whether actively engaging in corporate governance, benefiting from dividend payments, or advocating for changes as a minority shareholder, the rights and responsibilities associated with owning stocks play a crucial role in shaping the dynamics of the financial markets and the success of companies.

Section 3: How Stocks are Issued

The issuance of stocks is a crucial process in the lifecycle of a company and the stock market. It enables companies to raise capital, provides investors with opportunities to own a share of the company, and facilitates the trading of shares in secondary markets. This section delves into the various stages of stock issuance, including the Initial Public Offering (IPO) process, secondary markets and trading, and the mechanisms of share issuance and buybacks.

Initial Public Offering (IPO) Process

An Initial Public Offering (IPO) is the process by which a privately-held company offers its shares to the public for the first time. This process marks the transition from a private to a public company and involves several key steps:

1. **Preparation and Planning**
   Before an IPO, a company must prepare extensively. This preparation includes:

- **Choosing Underwriters:** The company selects investment banks or underwriters to manage the IPO process. These underwriters help determine the IPO price, structure the offering, and market the shares to potential investors.
- **Due Diligence:** The company and its underwriters conduct thorough due diligence, including reviewing financial statements, business operations, and legal matters. This process ensures that all relevant information is disclosed to potential investors.
- **Drafting the Prospectus:** A prospectus, or registration statement, is prepared and filed with the Securities and Exchange Commission (SEC) or the relevant regulatory body in the company's country. The prospectus includes detailed information about the company, its financials, management, business model, risks, and the terms of the offering.

2. **Regulatory Approval**
The IPO prospectus must be reviewed and approved by the regulatory authority before the company can proceed. This review process involves:

    - **SEC Review:** In the United States, the SEC reviews the registration statement to ensure compliance with securities laws and regulations. The SEC may request additional information or revisions before granting approval.

- **Regulatory Filings:** In other countries, similar regulatory bodies oversee the IPO process. Companies must comply with local regulations and provide required documentation.

3. **Marketing the IPO**
Once regulatory approval is obtained, the company and its underwriters begin marketing the IPO to potential investors. This phase includes:

    - **Roadshows:** The company's management team and underwriters conduct roadshows to present the company's investment case to institutional investors, analysts, and potential buyers. Roadshows are typically held in major financial centers and involve presentations, Q&A sessions, and meetings with potential investors.
    - **Book-Building:** During the book-building process, underwriters gauge investor interest and determine the optimal price range for the shares. Investors submit indications of interest, and the underwriters use this feedback to set the final offering price.

4. **Pricing and Allocation**
The final step in the IPO process is pricing and allocation:

    - **Pricing:** Based on investor demand and market conditions, the underwriters set the final IPO price. This price reflects the value of the company and the amount of capital it aims to raise.

- **Allocation:** Shares are allocated to investors based on their orders and the company's allocation strategy. Institutional investors often receive a significant portion of the shares, while retail investors may be allocated a smaller portion.

5. **Listing and Trading**
   After the IPO, the company's shares are listed on a stock exchange and begin trading publicly. This involves:
   - **Listing:** The company's shares are listed on a chosen stock exchange, such as the New York Stock Exchange (NYSE) or NASDAQ, where they can be bought and sold by the public.
   - **Trading:** The shares start trading on the exchange, with the initial trading price determined by supply and demand in the market. The stock price can fluctuate based on market conditions, investor sentiment, and company performance.

Secondary Markets and Trading

After the initial issuance of shares, the trading of stocks primarily occurs in secondary markets. These markets provide liquidity and enable investors to buy and sell shares after the IPO. Here's how secondary markets function:

1. **Role of Secondary Markets**
   Secondary markets are crucial for the functioning of financial markets. They provide a platform for investors to trade shares, allowing them to liquidate their holdings or acquire new ones. Key features include:

- **Liquidity:** Secondary markets enhance liquidity, enabling investors to buy and sell shares with relative ease. This liquidity is essential for maintaining investor confidence and market efficiency.
- **Price Discovery:** Trading in secondary markets helps establish the fair market value of a company's shares. Stock prices in secondary markets are determined by supply and demand dynamics and reflect investor perceptions of the company's value.

2. **Types of Secondary Markets**
Secondary markets can be categorized into different types based on trading mechanisms and participants:

    - **Stock Exchanges:** Major stock exchanges, such as the NYSE and NASDAQ, facilitate the trading of stocks in a regulated and transparent environment. These exchanges provide a centralized platform where buyers and sellers can transact.
    - **Over-the-Counter (OTC) Markets:** OTC markets, such as the OTC Bulletin Board (OTCBB) and Pink Sheets, offer a venue for trading stocks not listed on major exchanges. OTC markets often involve less regulation and may include smaller or emerging companies.
    - **Electronic Communication Networks (ECNs):** ECNs are automated platforms that match buy and sell orders for stocks. They provide an alternative

to traditional exchanges and offer extended trading hours.

3. **Trading Mechanisms**
   Secondary market trading involves various mechanisms and practices:

   - **Market Orders:** Investors place market orders to buy or sell shares at the current market price. Market orders are executed quickly but may experience price fluctuations due to market volatility.
   - **Limit Orders:** Limit orders specify a maximum or minimum price at which investors are willing to buy or sell shares. Limit orders are executed only if the stock price reaches the specified level, providing greater control over trade execution.
   - **Stop Orders:** Stop orders are used to trigger trades once a stock price reaches a certain level. Stop orders can be used to limit losses or secure profits.

4. **Role of Brokers and Market Makers**
   Brokers and market makers play essential roles in secondary markets:

   - **Brokers:** Brokers act as intermediaries between buyers and sellers, facilitating trades on behalf of their clients. They may charge commissions or fees for their services.
   - **Market Makers:** Market makers provide liquidity by quoting buy and sell prices for stocks and maintaining a continuous market. They help ensure

that there is a ready supply of shares available for trading.

Share Issuance and Buybacks

Share issuance and buybacks are important mechanisms that companies use to manage their capital structure and shareholder base. These processes impact stock availability, market capitalization, and shareholder value:

1. **Share Issuance**
   Companies may issue additional shares to raise capital for various purposes, including expansion, acquisitions, or debt repayment. The process involves:

    - **Public Offerings:** Companies can issue new shares through public offerings, similar to the IPO process but for companies that are already publicly traded. This includes follow-on offerings or secondary offerings.
    - **Private Placements:** Companies may also issue shares through private placements, where shares are sold directly to institutional investors or accredited individuals. Private placements are typically quicker and involve less regulatory scrutiny compared to public offerings.

   Share issuance can dilute existing shareholders' ownership stakes, as new shares increase the total number of shares outstanding. Companies must carefully consider the impact of dilution on shareholder value and stock price.

2. **Share Buybacks**
   Share buybacks, or share repurchases, involve a company buying back its own shares from the open market. This process has several motivations and effects:

   - **Reasons for Buybacks:** Companies may repurchase shares to return excess capital to shareholders, boost stock prices, or signal confidence in the company's future. Buybacks can also be used to offset dilution from employee stock options or acquisitions.
   - **Effects on Shareholders:** Share buybacks reduce the number of shares outstanding, potentially increasing earnings per share (EPS) and boosting the stock price. This can benefit remaining shareholders by increasing their ownership stake and the value of their holdings.

   Companies typically announce buyback programs and execute repurchases over time, either through open market purchases or tender offers. The impact of buybacks on stock price and shareholder value depends on market conditions and the company's financial health.

3. **Impact on Market Capitalization**
   Both share issuance and buybacks affect a company's market capitalization:

- **Issuance Impact:** Issuing new shares increases the total number of shares outstanding, which can impact the stock price and market capitalization. Companies must balance the need for capital with potential dilution effects.
- **Buyback Impact:** Share buybacks reduce the number of shares outstanding, potentially increasing the stock price and market capitalization. However, buybacks can also signal that the company lacks profitable investment opportunities or is seeking to manage stock price volatility.

The issuance of stocks is a multifaceted process involving the Initial Public Offering (IPO), secondary market trading, and mechanisms such as share issuance and buybacks. The IPO process marks the transition of a company to public status, providing a means for raising capital and increasing market visibility. Secondary markets facilitate the ongoing trading of shares, offering liquidity and price discovery for investors. Share issuance and buybacks allow companies to manage their capital structure and shareholder base, impacting stock availability and shareholder value.

Understanding these processes is crucial for investors, as they influence stock prices, market dynamics, and investment opportunities.

By comprehending the intricacies of stock issuance and trading, investors can better navigate the stock market and make informed decisions about their investments.

Chapter 3: Common vs. Preferred Stocks

Section 1: Differences Between Common and Preferred Stocks

In the world of stock investing, understanding the distinctions between common and preferred stocks is essential for making informed investment decisions. Each type of stock offers unique characteristics, benefits, and drawbacks, catering to different investor needs and goals. This section explores the key characteristics of common and preferred stocks, highlighting their primary features and the major differences between the two.

Key Characteristics of Common Stocks

Common stocks are the most prevalent type of stock issued by companies, representing ownership in a corporation and entitling shareholders to various rights and benefits. Here are the primary characteristics of common stocks:

1. **Ownership and Voting Rights**
    - **Ownership:** Common stockholders own a share of the company's equity, giving them a claim on the company's assets and earnings. Ownership is proportional to the number of shares held.
    - **Voting Rights:** Common shareholders typically have voting rights, allowing them to vote on important company matters, such as electing the board of directors and approving major corporate changes. Each share usually grants one vote, though the voting power may vary based on the company's structure.
2. **Dividend Payments**
    - **Dividend Payments:** Common stockholders may receive dividends, which are payments made by the company out of its profits. However, dividends on common stocks are not guaranteed and can fluctuate based on the company's financial performance and board decisions.
    - **Dividend Priority:** Common stockholders are last in line to receive dividends, as preferred stockholders and debt holders have priority. In

times of financial difficulty or company liquidation, common stockholders are paid only after all other claims have been settled.

3. **Capital Appreciation**
    - **Potential for Growth:** Common stocks have the potential for significant capital appreciation, as their value can increase with the company's growth and profitability. Shareholders benefit from rising stock prices and may realize gains by selling their shares at a higher price than the purchase price.
    - **Market Volatility:** The value of common stocks can be highly volatile, influenced by factors such as market conditions, company performance, and economic trends. This volatility can lead to substantial gains or losses for investors.
4. **Claim on Assets**
    - **Residual Claim:** In the event of liquidation, common stockholders have a residual claim on the company's assets. They are paid only after all debts and preferred stock dividends have been satisfied. This means that common stockholders face a higher risk compared to preferred stockholders and creditors.
5. **Liquidity and Marketability**
    - **Liquidity:** Common stocks are typically highly liquid and traded on major stock exchanges,

making them easily accessible for buying and selling. This liquidity provides investors with flexibility in managing their investments.

Features of Preferred Stocks

Preferred stocks are a hybrid form of equity that combines features of both common stocks and debt instruments. They offer different benefits and characteristics compared to common stocks:

1. **Fixed Dividends**
    - **Dividend Payments:** Preferred stocks typically offer fixed dividend payments, which are set at a specific rate and paid regularly. These dividends are usually higher than those of common stocks and are prioritized over common stock dividends.
    - **Dividend Priority:** Preferred stockholders receive dividends before common stockholders. In the event of a financial shortfall, preferred dividends must be paid before any dividends can be distributed to common shareholders.
2. **No Voting Rights**
    - **Lack of Voting Rights:** Preferred stockholders generally do not have voting rights. This means they do not participate in corporate governance decisions, such as electing the board of directors or voting on major corporate actions. Their

involvement is limited to financial matters related to their shares.

3. **Fixed or Adjustable Dividend Rates**
    - **Fixed Rates:** Many preferred stocks have fixed dividend rates, providing investors with predictable income. These rates are specified in the terms of the preferred stock issuance.
    - **Adjustable Rates:** Some preferred stocks feature adjustable dividend rates that can change based on market conditions or specified benchmarks. Adjustable rates may offer investors a chance to benefit from changing interest rates.
4. **Convertible Features**
    - **Convertibility:** Certain preferred stocks come with conversion features, allowing holders to convert their preferred shares into a specified number of common shares. This feature provides potential for capital appreciation if the company performs well.
5. **Callable and Redeemable**
    - **Callable:** Preferred stocks may be callable, meaning the issuing company has the right to repurchase the shares at a predetermined price before the maturity date. Callable features allow companies to refinance or restructure their capital if advantageous.

- **Redeemable:** Preferred shares may also be redeemable, which means the company can redeem (buy back) the shares at a specified price, providing an exit option for investors.

6. **Preference in Liquidation**

    - **Liquidation Preference:** In the event of liquidation, preferred stockholders have a higher claim on the company's assets than common stockholders. They are paid after debt holders but before common shareholders, reducing their risk compared to common stockholders.

Major Differences Between Common and Preferred Stocks

The primary differences between common and preferred stocks lie in their rights, dividends, and risk profiles. Understanding these differences helps investors choose the type of stock that aligns with their financial goals and risk tolerance:

1. **Dividend Payments and Priority**

    - **Common Stocks:** Dividends are variable and depend on the company's performance. Common stockholders receive dividends only after preferred stockholders have been paid.
    - **Preferred Stocks:** Dividends are fixed and have priority over common stock dividends. Preferred stockholders receive regular, predictable income before common stockholders.

2. **Voting Rights**

- **Common Stocks:** Provide voting rights, allowing shareholders to participate in corporate governance and decision-making processes.
- **Preferred Stocks:** Generally do not provide voting rights, limiting shareholders' influence on corporate matters.

3. **Dividend Stability and Income**

- **Common Stocks:** Dividend payments can be inconsistent and are subject to the company's financial health and decisions by the board of directors.
- **Preferred Stocks:** Offer stable and predictable dividend payments, often making them more attractive to income-focused investors.

4. **Claim on Assets in Liquidation**

- **Common Stocks:** Have a residual claim on assets, meaning they are paid after all other claims have been settled. This results in higher risk for common stockholders in liquidation scenarios.
- **Preferred Stocks:** Have a higher claim on assets compared to common stockholders, providing a lower-risk profile in liquidation situations.

5. **Capital Appreciation Potential**

- **Common Stocks:** Offer potential for significant capital appreciation if the company performs well, as their value can increase with the company's success.

- **Preferred Stocks:** Generally have limited potential for capital appreciation. They are designed more for stable income rather than significant growth.

6. **Market Volatility**

- **Common Stocks:** Subject to market volatility and fluctuations based on company performance and broader economic conditions.
- **Preferred Stocks:** Typically less volatile than common stocks, as their value is influenced more by interest rates and fixed income features.

Common and preferred stocks offer distinct characteristics and benefits, catering to different investment strategies and risk profiles. Common stocks provide ownership with voting rights, potential for capital appreciation, and variable dividends. They come with higher risk and potential for significant returns based on the company's performance. Preferred stocks, on the other hand, offer fixed dividends, priority in dividend payments and liquidation, and reduced volatility, making them suitable for investors seeking stable income and lower risk.

Understanding these differences is crucial for investors as they build their portfolios and make investment decisions. By selecting the appropriate type of stock, investors can align their investments with their financial goals, risk tolerance, and income requirements, ultimately enhancing their overall investment strategy.

Section 2: Pros and Cons of Each Type

When evaluating investment options in the stock market, understanding the advantages and disadvantages of common and preferred stocks is crucial. Each type of stock offers distinct benefits and potential drawbacks, making them suitable for different investment goals and risk profiles. This section delves into the pros and cons of both common and preferred stocks, and explores which type may be best suited for various investment objectives.

Advantages and Disadvantages of Common Stocks

Advantages:

1. **Potential for High Capital Appreciation**
    - **Growth Opportunities:** Common stocks offer significant potential for capital appreciation. If the company performs well, its stock price can increase substantially, providing investors with the opportunity to achieve high returns. The value of common shares is directly linked to the company's growth and profitability.
    - **Dividends:** While not guaranteed, common stockholders may receive dividends, which can grow over time as the company expands and becomes more profitable. This potential for increasing dividend payments adds to the attractiveness of common stocks.
2. **Voting Rights and Corporate Influence**

- **Participation in Governance:** Common stockholders typically have voting rights, allowing them to participate in key corporate decisions, such as electing board members and approving major transactions. This involvement provides shareholders with a voice in the company's direction and management.
- **Influence on Corporate Actions:** Voting rights enable shareholders to influence corporate actions and decisions that may impact their investments, fostering a sense of ownership and engagement in the company's success.

3. **Liquidity and Market Accessibility**

    - **High Liquidity:** Common stocks are generally traded on major stock exchanges, offering high liquidity and ease of trading. Investors can buy or sell shares quickly, providing flexibility in managing their investment positions.
    - **Broad Market Access:** The widespread availability of common stocks on various exchanges makes them accessible to a broad range of investors, from retail to institutional.

Disadvantages:

1. **Higher Volatility and Risk**

    - **Market Fluctuations:** Common stocks are subject to market volatility and fluctuations in stock prices. The value of common shares can be influenced by a range of factors, including market sentiment, economic conditions, and company performance, leading to potential gains or losses.

- **Financial Risk:** Common stockholders bear the risk of financial loss if the company underperforms or faces economic challenges. In the event of company liquidation, common shareholders are last in line to receive any remaining assets, making them more vulnerable to financial losses.

2. **Dividend Uncertainty**

    - **Variable Dividends:** Dividends on common stocks are not guaranteed and can vary based on the company's financial performance and board decisions. In times of economic downturn or financial difficulty, companies may reduce or eliminate dividend payments, affecting investors' income.

3. **Lower Priority in Bankruptcy**

    - **Residual Claims:** In the event of bankruptcy or liquidation, common stockholders have a residual claim on the company's assets. They are paid only after all other claims, such as debt holders and preferred stockholders, have been settled. This lower priority increases the risk of not receiving any return on their investment in adverse situations.

Pros and Cons of Preferred Stocks

Advantages:

1. **Fixed and Predictable Dividends**
    - **Stable Income:** Preferred stocks offer fixed dividend payments, providing investors with predictable and regular income. This stability makes preferred stocks an attractive option for income-focused investors seeking consistent returns.
    - **Priority Dividends:** Preferred stockholders receive dividends before common stockholders, ensuring that they are paid first if the company distributes profits. This priority adds a layer of security to the income stream from preferred stocks.
2. **Reduced Volatility**
    - **Price Stability:** Preferred stocks are generally less volatile than common stocks, as their value is influenced more by interest rates and fixed income features rather than company performance and market conditions. This reduced volatility provides a more stable investment experience.
    - **Lower Risk:** The fixed dividend payments and higher claim on assets in liquidation contribute to a lower risk profile compared to common stocks. Preferred stockholders are less exposed to significant price fluctuations and financial losses.

3. **Convertible Features**
    - **Potential for Upside:** Some preferred stocks come with conversion features that allow holders to convert their shares into common stock at specified terms. This convertibility provides potential for capital appreciation if the company's common stock performs well.

Disadvantages:

1. **Limited Capital Appreciation**
    - **Capped Growth:** Preferred stocks generally have limited potential for capital appreciation compared to common stocks. Their value is more closely tied to fixed dividend payments and interest rates rather than significant price increases.
    - **Less Growth Opportunity:** Preferred stockholders miss out on the potential for substantial gains associated with the company's growth and success. The fixed dividend and limited price appreciation can restrict overall investment returns.
2. **Lack of Voting Rights**
    - **No Corporate Influence:** Preferred stockholders typically do not have voting rights, meaning they cannot participate in corporate governance or influence major company decisions. This lack of involvement can be a disadvantage for investors who wish to have a say in the company's direction.

3. **Callable and Redeemable Risks**

    - **Callable Risks:** Some preferred stocks are callable, allowing the issuing company to repurchase the shares at a predetermined price before maturity. This feature can be disadvantageous if the shares are called away when market conditions are favorable for the investor.
    - **Redeemable Risks:** Redeemable preferred stocks can be bought back by the company at a specified price, which may limit the investor's ability to benefit from future price appreciation or steady income.

Which Type Suits Different Investment Goals?

Choosing between common and preferred stocks depends on individual investment goals, risk tolerance, and income preferences. Each type of stock serves different purposes and aligns with various investment strategies:

1. **Growth-Oriented Investors**

    - **Preference for Common Stocks:** Investors seeking capital appreciation and growth potential should consider common stocks. These stocks offer the opportunity for significant price increases as the company expands and performs well. Common stocks are suitable for those with a higher risk tolerance and a long-term investment horizon.

2. **Income-Focused Investors**
   - **Preference for Preferred Stocks:** Investors prioritizing stable income and predictable returns may find preferred stocks more suitable. The fixed dividend payments and reduced volatility of preferred stocks provide a steady income stream, making them ideal for income-focused portfolios and retirees seeking reliable cash flow.
3. **Balanced Investors**
   - **Diversified Approach:** Investors who aim for a balanced portfolio may choose to invest in both common and preferred stocks. This approach allows for a mix of growth potential and income stability, accommodating varying investment goals and risk profiles.
4. **Risk-Averse Investors**
   - **Preference for Preferred Stocks:** For those with a lower risk tolerance, preferred stocks offer a safer investment option due to their fixed dividends and higher claim on assets. The reduced volatility and income stability can provide a sense of security in uncertain market conditions.
5. **Long-Term Investors**
   - **Preference for Common Stocks:** Long-term investors who are willing to weather market

fluctuations and aim for substantial growth may favor common stocks. The potential for significant capital appreciation over time aligns with long-term investment strategies.

6. **Income Needs and Liquidity**

    - **Preference for Preferred Stocks:** Investors needing regular income and lower volatility may prefer preferred stocks. The fixed dividends and priority payments address the need for consistent cash flow while minimizing exposure to market swings.

Understanding the pros and cons of common and preferred stocks is essential for making informed investment decisions. Common stocks offer potential for high capital appreciation, voting rights, and liquidity, but come with higher volatility and risk. Preferred stocks provide fixed dividends, reduced volatility, and priority in payments, but have limited capital appreciation and lack voting rights.

By aligning investment choices with individual goals, risk tolerance, and income needs, investors can select the type of stock that best fits their financial objectives. Whether seeking growth, stable income, or a balanced approach, understanding these stock types empowers investors to build a well-rounded and effective investment portfolio.

Section 3: Voting Rights and Dividends

When investing in stocks, understanding the nuances of voting rights and dividends is critical, as these elements significantly impact investor control and income. This section provides a detailed exploration of the voting privileges associated with common stockholders, the dividend payments for preferred stocks, and how dividends affect stock value. Additionally, it includes charts and tables to illustrate these concepts clearly.

Voting Privileges of Common Stockholders

Common stockholders typically enjoy several key privileges that contribute to their influence over corporate governance:

1. **Voting Rights Overview**
    - **Shareholder Meetings:** Common stockholders have the right to vote at annual general meetings (AGMs) and special meetings. These meetings cover significant corporate issues, such as electing the board of directors, approving major mergers or acquisitions, and making amendments to the company's charter or bylaws.
    - **One Share, One Vote:** Generally, each common share grants one vote. However, some companies issue dual-class shares with different voting rights, where certain shares may have multiple votes per share while others may have none.
2. **Impact on Corporate Governance**
    - **Board Elections:** Common stockholders vote to elect members of the board of directors, who are

responsible for overseeing the company's management and strategic decisions. The election process ensures that shareholders have a say in who represents their interests.

- **Major Decisions:** Voting rights extend to critical decisions such as approving significant capital expenditures, altering corporate structures, and other major changes that could impact shareholder value.

3. **Proxy Voting**

- **Proxy Forms:** If common stockholders cannot attend meetings in person, they can vote by proxy. Proxy voting allows shareholders to appoint someone else to vote on their behalf using a proxy form.
- **Electronic Voting:** Many companies offer electronic voting options, making it easier for shareholders to participate in the voting process without physical presence.

Table 1: Common Stockholder Voting Rights

Voting Right	Description	Impact on Shareholders
Annual General Meetings (AGMs)	Voting on routine matters, including board elections.	Influence on board composition and corporate governance.
Special Meetings	Voting on specific issues, such as mergers	Direct impact on strategic decisions and

Voting Right	Description	Impact on Shareholders
	and acquisitions.	company direction.
Proxy Voting	Voting via a designated representative.	Enables participation without physical attendance.
Electronic Voting	Online voting option for AGMs and special meetings.	Facilitates easier and more accessible voting.

Dividend Payments for Preferred Stocks

Preferred stocks are known for their fixed dividend payments, which provide a stable income stream for investors. Here's an overview of how dividends work for preferred stocks:

1. **Fixed Dividend Rates**
    - **Dividend Amount:** Preferred stocks usually offer a fixed dividend rate, expressed as a percentage of the stock's par value or face value. This rate is specified at the time of issuance and provides predictable income.
    - **Payment Schedule:** Dividends are typically paid quarterly, although some preferred stocks may offer monthly or annual payments. The fixed nature of these dividends ensures a stable cash flow for investors.
2. **Dividend Priority**
    - **Payment Order:** Preferred stockholders receive dividends before common stockholders. If a

company faces financial difficulties and decides to suspend dividends, preferred stockholders are paid first, and common stockholders may not receive any dividends until preferred dividends are fully paid.

- **Cumulative vs. Non-Cumulative:** Cumulative preferred stocks have a feature where unpaid dividends accumulate and must be paid out before any dividends can be paid to common stockholders. Non-cumulative preferred stocks do not have this feature, meaning missed dividend payments are not recovered.

3. **Dividend Adjustments and Callable Features**

- **Adjustable Dividends:** Some preferred stocks offer adjustable dividend rates that can change based on prevailing interest rates or other benchmarks. This feature can benefit investors in a rising interest rate environment.
- **Callable Preferred Stocks:** Companies may have the right to call (repurchase) preferred stocks at a predetermined price. If the stock is called, the investor receives the call price and may lose future dividend income.

Chart 1: Fixed vs. Adjustable Preferred Stock Dividends

Type of Preferred Stock	Dividend Feature	Impact on Investor Income
Fixed Dividend	Set rate based on par value.	Stable and predictable income.

Type of Preferred Stock	Dividend Feature	Impact on Investor Income
Adjustable Dividend	Rate changes with interest rates.	Potentially higher income in rising rate environments.

How Dividends Affect Stock Value

Dividends play a significant role in determining a stock's value, affecting both common and preferred stocks in different ways:

1. **Impact on Common Stock Value**
   - **Dividend Discount Model (DDM):** Common stock value is often assessed using the Dividend Discount Model, which calculates the present value of expected future dividends. The model assumes that dividends grow at a constant rate and discounts them to their present value.
   - **Market Perception:** Regular and growing dividend payments can positively influence investor perception and demand, leading to higher stock prices. Conversely, the suspension or reduction of dividends may lead to decreased stock prices due to negative market sentiment.
2. **Impact on Preferred Stock Value**
   - **Fixed Income Feature:** The fixed dividend payments of preferred stocks are similar to interest payments on bonds. The value of preferred stocks is influenced by changes in interest rates. When

interest rates rise, the fixed dividends become less attractive, leading to a decline in the stock's value. Conversely, falling interest rates can increase the value of preferred stocks.

- **Callability and Redemption:** Preferred stocks with callable features may be repurchased by the issuing company at a set price, affecting their market value. Investors must consider the possibility of early redemption when assessing the stock's value.

Table 2: How Dividends Affect Stock Value

Stock Type	Effect of Dividends on Value	Factors Influencing Value
Common Stocks	Higher or stable dividends can increase stock price; reductions or suspensions can lower it.	Market perception, company performance, dividend growth rates.
Preferred Stocks	Fixed dividends may lead to decreased value if interest rates rise; increased value if rates fall.	Interest rates, callability, fixed income stability.

Understanding the voting rights and dividend characteristics of common and preferred stocks is crucial for making informed investment decisions. Common stockholders benefit from voting privileges that allow them to influence corporate governance and have the potential for significant capital appreciation and variable dividends. Preferred stockholders enjoy fixed and predictable dividends, with priority over common stockholders but lack voting rights.

The impact of dividends on stock value varies between common and preferred stocks, influenced by factors such as interest rates and market perception. By recognizing these differences, investors can align their investment choices with their financial goals, whether seeking influence over corporate decisions, stable income, or potential growth.

Understanding these elements helps investors make informed choices, ensuring their investment strategies align with their financial objectives and risk tolerance.

Chapter 4: The Importance of Risk and Volatility

Section 1: Understanding Risk in Investing

Understanding risk is fundamental to successful investing. In the context of stock investing, risk refers to the possibility of losing some or all of an investment's value. It is crucial for investors to comprehend various types of risks, the factors influencing these risks, and how to assess their own risk tolerance. This section provides an in-depth exploration of different types of risks in stock investing, including market risk, credit risk, and other factors, as well as guidance on risk tolerance assessment.

Types of Risks in Stock Investing

Investing in stocks involves several types of risks, each with its own characteristics and implications. Below are the key types of risks associated with stock investing:

1. **Market Risk**

    - **Definition:** Market risk, also known as systematic risk, refers to the risk of losses due to overall market movements. This type of risk affects all stocks and is influenced by macroeconomic factors such as economic downturns, political instability, interest rate changes, and natural disasters.
    - **Examples:** A stock market crash, recession, or geopolitical tensions can lead to significant declines in stock prices across the board. Market risk cannot be eliminated through diversification but can be managed through strategic asset allocation.

2. **Credit Risk**

    - **Definition:** Credit risk pertains to the risk of a company defaulting on its financial obligations, such as interest payments or principal repayment. This risk is more relevant to bond investors but can also affect stockholders if a company faces financial distress or bankruptcy.
    - **Examples:** If a company's credit rating is downgraded, its stock price may fall due to increased perceived risk of default. Credit risk is closely related to a company's financial health and ability to meet its debt obligations.

3. **Liquidity Risk**

- **Definition:** Liquidity risk involves the risk of being unable to buy or sell a stock quickly without significantly affecting its price. Stocks with low trading volumes or those in less liquid markets can be harder to sell without incurring substantial losses.
- **Examples:** Investing in small-cap stocks or stocks that are not frequently traded can lead to difficulties in executing trades at desired prices, particularly in volatile market conditions.

4. **Business Risk**

- **Definition:** Business risk refers to the risk associated with the specific operational and financial activities of a company. It includes factors such as poor management decisions, competitive pressures, and operational inefficiencies.
- **Examples:** A company experiencing declining revenues, increased costs, or losing market share may face business risk that impacts its stock performance. Business risk is unique to each company and can be mitigated through thorough research and analysis.

5. **Interest Rate Risk**

- **Definition:** Interest rate risk is the risk that changes in interest rates will affect the value of investments. For stocks, this risk manifests when rising interest rates lead to higher borrowing costs and reduced consumer spending, potentially impacting company earnings.

- **Examples:** A company with significant debt may experience higher interest expenses during periods of rising interest rates, which can negatively affect its stock price.

6. **Inflation Risk**

- **Definition:** Inflation risk refers to the risk that rising inflation will erode the purchasing power of future cash flows. For stocks, this can mean reduced real returns if the rate of inflation exceeds the growth rate of a company's earnings.
- **Examples:** High inflation can lead to increased costs for companies and reduced consumer spending, impacting corporate profits and stock valuations.

Table 1: Types of Risks in Stock Investing

Type of Risk	Definition	Examples	Impact on Stocks
Market Risk	Risk due to overall market movements.	Market crashes, economic downturns.	Affects all stocks; cannot be eliminated through diversification.
Credit Risk	Risk of default on financial obligations by a company.	Downgrade in credit rating, bankruptcy.	Leads to declines in stock prices due to perceived risk.
Liquidity	Risk of difficulty	Low trading	Results in

Type of Risk	Definition	Examples	Impact on Stocks
Risk	in buying or selling stocks without affecting price.	volume, less liquid stocks.	potential losses during trade execution.
Business Risk	Risk associated with a company's operations and financial activities.	Poor management decisions, competitive pressures.	Impacts individual company stock performance.
Interest Rate Risk	Risk that changes in interest rates will affect stock values.	Rising borrowing costs, reduced consumer spending.	Can impact company earnings and stock prices.
Inflation Risk	Risk that inflation will erode purchasing power of returns.	Increased costs, reduced consumer spending.	Affects real returns and stock valuations.

Market Risk, Credit Risk, and Other Factors

Market Risk

Market risk is inherent in all stock investments and stems from external factors affecting the entire market. To manage market risk, investors use strategies such as diversification, asset allocation, and hedging. Diversification across different asset classes, sectors, and geographical regions can help mitigate the impact of market downturns on an investment portfolio.

Credit Risk

Credit risk affects stocks indirectly through the financial stability of the issuing company. While stockholders are not directly impacted by credit risk in the same way bondholders are, a company's creditworthiness can influence its stock price. Investors should assess a company's financial health, including its debt levels and credit ratings, to gauge credit risk.

Liquidity Risk

Liquidity risk is a significant consideration for investors trading less frequently traded stocks or those in smaller markets. Stocks with higher trading volumes generally offer better liquidity, allowing investors to buy and sell shares without significant price impacts. Investing in liquid stocks or using limit orders can help manage liquidity risk.

Business Risk

Business risk is specific to individual companies and involves analyzing their operational and financial performance. Investors should evaluate factors such as management effectiveness, competitive landscape, and industry trends to assess business risk. Thorough research and due diligence can help identify and mitigate business risk.

Interest Rate Risk

Interest rate risk affects stocks through its impact on borrowing costs and consumer spending. Companies with high levels of debt are more sensitive to interest rate changes. Investors should monitor interest rate trends and consider how they might affect companies' earnings and stock prices.

Inflation Risk

Inflation risk can erode the purchasing power of future returns. Companies with pricing power and the ability to pass on costs to consumers are better positioned to handle inflation. Investors should consider how inflation might impact a company's profitability and adjust their portfolios accordingly.

Chart 1: Risk Factors and Their Impact on Stocks

Risk Factor	Impact on Stocks	Management Strategies
Market Risk	Affects all stocks; potential for broad market declines.	Diversification, asset allocation, hedging.
Credit Risk	Influences stock prices through company financial health.	Assess company credit ratings and debt levels.
Liquidity Risk	Difficulty in executing trades at desired prices.	Invest in liquid stocks, use limit orders.
Business Risk	Affects individual stock performance based on	Conduct thorough research and analysis.

Risk Factor	Impact on Stocks	Management Strategies
	company operations.	
Interest Rate Risk	Impacts borrowing costs and consumer spending.	Monitor interest rate trends, adjust investments.
Inflation Risk	Erodes real returns, impacts company profitability.	Invest in companies with pricing power, adjust for inflation.

Risk Tolerance Assessment

Assessing risk tolerance is essential for creating an investment strategy that aligns with an investor's financial goals, time horizon, and comfort level with risk. Risk tolerance refers to an investor's ability and willingness to endure market volatility and potential losses.

1. **Assessing Risk Tolerance**

    - **Financial Goals:** Determine investment objectives, such as retirement savings, wealth accumulation, or income generation. Different goals may require different risk levels.
    - **Time Horizon:** Consider the length of time an investor plans to hold investments before needing to access the funds. Longer time horizons generally allow for higher risk tolerance due to the ability to recover from short-term volatility.
    - **Investment Experience:** Evaluate an investor's experience and knowledge of the stock market. More experienced investors may be comfortable

with higher risk, while less experienced investors may prefer a conservative approach.

- **Financial Situation:** Assess the investor's current financial situation, including income, expenses, and existing investments. A stable financial situation may support a higher risk tolerance.

2. **Risk Tolerance Questionnaires**

    - **Purpose:** Risk tolerance questionnaires are tools designed to assess an investor's risk appetite and guide them in selecting appropriate investments. These questionnaires consider various factors such as financial goals, investment experience, and emotional response to market fluctuations.
    - **Example Questions:** Typical questions may include:
        - How would you react to a significant drop in the value of your investments?
        - What is your primary investment goal (e.g., growth, income, preservation)?
        - How long do you plan to invest before needing access to your funds?

3. **Adjusting Risk Tolerance**

    - **Periodic Reviews:** Risk tolerance may change over time due to shifts in financial goals, market conditions, or personal circumstances. Investors should periodically review and adjust their risk tolerance and investment strategy accordingly.

- **Diversification:** Adjusting asset allocation and diversification can help manage risk within a portfolio. A well-diversified portfolio can balance risk and return based on the investor's risk tolerance.

Table 2: Risk Tolerance Assessment Factors

Factor	Consideration	Impact on Risk Tolerance
Financial Goals	Determine objectives such as growth or income.	Influences risk level needed to achieve goals.
Time Horizon	Length of investment period before accessing funds.	Longer horizons allow for higher risk tolerance.
Investment Experience	Level of experience with market volatility.	Experienced investors may accept higher risk.
Financial Situation	Current income, expenses, and investments.	A stable situation supports higher risk tolerance.

Understanding risk is vital for effective stock investing. Market risk, credit risk, liquidity risk, business risk, interest rate risk, and inflation risk each have unique implications for stock investments. By recognizing these risks and implementing appropriate management strategies, investors can better navigate the complexities of the stock market.

Assessing risk tolerance is equally important, ensuring that investment strategies align with individual financial goals, time horizons, and risk comfort levels. Using tools such as risk tolerance questionnaires and regularly reviewing investment strategies helps investors stay on track and make informed decisions.

Incorporating a thorough understanding of risk and risk tolerance into investment planning allows investors to build portfolios that are well-suited to their needs, ultimately supporting long-term financial success and stability.

Section 2: How Volatility Affects Stock Prices

Volatility is a fundamental concept in investing that can significantly impact stock prices and investor behavior. This section delves into what volatility is, how it is measured, and its effects on both short-term and long-term investors. Understanding these aspects can help investors navigate market fluctuations and make informed decisions.

What is Volatility?

Volatility refers to the degree of variation in a stock's price over time. It is a measure of how much the price of a security, such as a stock, fluctuates from its average price. High volatility indicates larger price swings and greater uncertainty, while low volatility reflects smaller price changes and more stability.

1. **Definition and Importance**

    - **Price Fluctuations:** Volatility represents the extent to which a stock's price deviates from its mean or average price. Stocks with high volatility experience significant price changes in short periods, while those with low volatility have more stable prices.

- **Investor Perception:** Investors often view high volatility as a sign of increased risk but also potential for higher returns. Conversely, low volatility is perceived as less risky but may offer lower returns. Understanding volatility helps investors assess the risk-reward profile of their investments.

2. **Sources of Volatility**

- **Market Conditions:** Broader market conditions, such as economic data releases, geopolitical events, and changes in interest rates, can drive volatility. Market-wide events can lead to widespread price movements and increased uncertainty.
- **Company-Specific Factors:** Volatility can also arise from company-specific news, such as earnings reports, management changes, or regulatory issues. Unexpected developments in a company's performance can lead to significant price swings.

3. **Impact on Investment Strategy**

- **Risk Management:** Investors need to consider volatility when developing their investment strategies. High volatility may require more cautious approaches, such as diversification and hedging, to manage potential risks. Low volatility environments might allow for more aggressive strategies.

- **Opportunity for Traders:** For short-term traders, high volatility presents opportunities for profit through quick trades. However, it also increases the risk of losses if market movements are unpredictable.

Chart 1: Understanding Volatility

Volatility Level	Price Fluctuations	Investor Perception	Investment Implications
High	Large swings in price	Higher risk but potential for higher returns	May require cautious strategies; opportunities for traders.
Low	Small swings in price	Lower risk with potentially lower returns	Allows for more aggressive strategies; less risk.

Measuring Volatility

Several tools and metrics are used to measure and quantify volatility. Two of the most common measures are the VIX and beta.

1. **VIX (Volatility Index)**
    - **Definition:** The VIX, often referred to as the "fear gauge," is a measure of market volatility derived from the prices of S&P 500 index options. It

reflects the market's expectations of future volatility over the next 30 days.

- **Calculation:** The VIX is calculated using the implied volatilities of a wide range of S&P 500 options. It represents the market's consensus forecast of future volatility based on option prices.
- **Interpretation:** A higher VIX value indicates greater expected market volatility, often associated with increased investor anxiety and uncertainty. A lower VIX suggests lower expected volatility and a more stable market environment.

Chart 2: VIX Index and Market Volatility

Note: This is a placeholder. Replace with actual VIX chart.

VIX Value	Market Condition	Investor Sentiment
High	Increased market volatility	Increased fear and uncertainty.
Low	Reduced market volatility	Increased confidence and stability.

2. **Beta**
    - **Definition:** Beta is a measure of a stock's volatility relative to the overall market. It indicates how much a stock's price is expected to move in relation to market movements.
    - **Calculation:** Beta is calculated by comparing the historical price movements of a stock to those of a market index, such as the S&P 500. A beta of 1

indicates that the stock's price moves in line with the market, while a beta greater than 1 signifies higher volatility, and a beta less than 1 indicates lower volatility.

- **Interpretation:** Investors use beta to assess a stock's risk in relation to the market. A higher beta stock is more sensitive to market movements and may offer higher potential returns along with greater risk. Conversely, a lower beta stock is less sensitive to market fluctuations and typically presents lower risk.

Table 1: Beta Values and Volatility

Beta Value	Stock Volatility Relative to Market	Investment Implications
>1	Higher volatility compared to the market	Higher potential returns with higher risk.
=1	Volatility in line with the market	Reflects overall market risk.
<1	Lower volatility compared to the market	Lower risk with potentially lower returns.

Impact on Short-Term vs. Long-Term Investors

Volatility affects investors differently based on their investment horizons and strategies.

1. **Short-Term Investors**
   - **Trading Opportunities:** Short-term investors, such as day traders and swing traders, often seek to capitalize on short-term price fluctuations. High

volatility can provide trading opportunities, as significant price movements can lead to profitable trades.

- **Increased Risk:** While high volatility can create opportunities, it also increases the risk of losses. Short-term investors must be vigilant and responsive to market changes to manage risk effectively.
- **Technical Analysis:** Short-term investors frequently use technical analysis, including chart patterns and technical indicators, to make trading decisions. High volatility can lead to more frequent signals and patterns that traders use to execute trades.

Chart 3: Short-Term Trading Strategy

Volatility Level	Trading Opportunities	Risk Management	Technical Analysis
High	More frequent price movements	Requires active monitoring and quick decisions.	Increased signals and patterns.
Low	Fewer price movements	Generally more stable but less frequent trading opportunities.	Fewer signals and patterns.

2. **Long-Term Investors**
    - **Impact of Volatility:** Long-term investors, such as retirement savers and buy-and-hold investors, are generally less affected by short-term volatility.

Their focus is on the long-term growth potential of their investments rather than short-term price fluctuations.

- **Risk Tolerance:** Long-term investors can often tolerate higher levels of volatility, as they have the time to recover from market downturns. They benefit from the compounding effect and can ride out market volatility over time.
- **Diversification:** Long-term investors often employ diversification strategies to mitigate the impact of volatility. By spreading investments across different asset classes and sectors, they can reduce the overall risk of their portfolios.

Table 2: Impact of Volatility on Investment Horizons

Investment Horizon	Response to Volatility	Strategy	Risk Management
Short-Term	Actively responds to price changes	Frequent trading, technical analysis.	Requires close monitoring and quick adjustments.
Long-Term	Less impacted by short-term fluctuations	Focus on long-term growth, buy-and-hold.	Employs diversification and long-term perspective.

Understanding volatility is crucial for navigating the stock market and making informed investment decisions. Volatility represents the degree of price fluctuations and affects both short-term and long-term investors differently. Measuring tools like the VIX and beta provide insights into market and stock-specific volatility, helping investors assess risk and potential returns.

For short-term investors, high volatility presents opportunities for profit but also increases risk. Effective risk management and technical analysis are essential for capitalizing on short-term price movements. Long-term investors, on the other hand, can weather short-term volatility by focusing on long-term growth and employing diversification strategies.

By comprehending how volatility impacts stock prices and aligning investment strategies with personal risk tolerance and goals, investors can better navigate market fluctuations and enhance their potential for financial success.

Section 3: Managing Risk as a Beginner Investor

Managing risk is a crucial aspect of investing, especially for beginners who are just starting to build their portfolios. Understanding and implementing effective risk management strategies can help protect investments from significant losses and ensure long-term financial success. This section explores key risk management strategies, the role of diversification and asset allocation, and the importance of setting realistic investment expectations.

Risk Management Strategies

1. **Diversification**

    - **Definition:** Diversification is the practice of spreading investments across a wide range of assets to reduce exposure to any single asset or risk. The primary goal is to minimize the impact of poor performance in any one investment on the overall portfolio.

- **Types of Diversification:**
    - **Asset Class Diversification:** Invest in different asset classes such as stocks, bonds, real estate, and cash. Each asset class behaves differently under various market conditions, helping to balance risk.
    - **Sector Diversification:** Within the stock market, diversify across various sectors such as technology, healthcare, finance, and consumer goods. Different sectors may perform differently based on economic cycles.
    - **Geographical Diversification:** Invest in domestic and international markets to mitigate risks associated with economic or political issues in a specific country or region.
- **Example:** A diversified portfolio might include 40% stocks, 30% bonds, 20% real estate, and 10% cash. This allocation reduces the risk that any single asset class will significantly impact the overall portfolio.

Table 1: Diversification Strategy

Asset Class	Percentage of Portfolio	Purpose
Stocks	40%	Growth and potential high returns
Bonds	30%	Income and stability
Real Estate	20%	Income and diversification
Cash	10%	Liquidity and safety

2. **Asset Allocation**
    - **Definition:** Asset allocation refers to the process of deciding how to distribute investments among different asset classes. It aims to balance risk and reward based on an investor's financial goals, risk tolerance, and investment horizon.
    - **Types of Asset Allocation:**
        - **Strategic Allocation:** Long-term allocation based on investor's goals and risk tolerance. Adjustments are made periodically based on changing goals or market conditions.
        - **Tactical Allocation:** Short-term adjustments made to capitalize on market opportunities or to respond to economic changes. It involves actively managing the allocation based on market trends.
    - **Example:** A conservative investor might have 70% bonds and 30% stocks, while a more aggressive investor might have 80% stocks and 20% bonds.

The choice depends on the investor's risk tolerance and investment goals.

Chart 1: Asset Allocation Models
Note: This is a placeholder. Replace with actual asset allocation chart.

Investor Type	Stocks	Bonds	Real Estate	Cash	Purpose
Conservative	30%	60%	5%	5%	Income and low risk
Balanced	50%	40%	5%	5%	Balanced risk and return
Aggressive	70%	20%	5%	5%	High growth potential

3. **Setting Realistic Investment Expectations**

   - **Understanding Return Expectations:** It's important to have realistic expectations about the returns on investments. Historical performance data can provide a benchmark, but future returns can vary based on market conditions and economic factors.
   - **Time Horizon:** Your investment time horizon—the period over which you plan to hold your investments before needing access to the funds—affects your risk tolerance and expected returns. Longer time horizons generally allow for more risk-taking, as there is more time to recover from market fluctuations.

- **Risk Tolerance:** Assessing your own risk tolerance helps in setting realistic investment goals. Understanding your comfort level with potential losses and gains is crucial for setting achievable expectations and avoiding panic during market downturns.

Table 2: Setting Realistic Expectations

Practical Tips for Beginner Investors

1. **Start Small and Gradually Increase Exposure**
    - **Initial Investment:** Begin with a small amount of money and gradually increase your investment as you gain more confidence and understanding of the market.
    - **Learning Curve:** Use the initial investments as a learning experience to understand how different assets behave and how market conditions affect your portfolio.
2. **Regularly Review and Rebalance Your Portfolio**
    - **Periodic Reviews:** Regularly review your investment portfolio to ensure it aligns with your financial goals and risk tolerance. Adjustments may be needed based on changes in market conditions or personal circumstances.
    - **Rebalancing:** Rebalance your portfolio periodically to maintain your desired asset

allocation. This involves buying or selling assets to return to your target allocation percentages.

3. **Avoid Emotional Investing**
    - **Stay Disciplined:** Avoid making investment decisions based on emotions or short-term market movements. Stick to your investment plan and focus on long-term goals.
    - **Stay Informed:** Keep yourself informed about market trends and economic conditions but avoid reacting impulsively to news or market fluctuations.

Chart 2: Investment Tips for Beginners

Note: This is a placeholder. Replace with actual investment tips chart.

Tip	Explanation
Start Small	Begin with small investments and increase gradually.
Regular Reviews	Review and adjust your portfolio periodically.
Avoid Emotional Investing	Make decisions based on your plan, not emotions.

Managing risk effectively is essential for beginner investors to protect their investments and achieve their financial goals. By implementing strategies such as diversification, asset allocation, and setting realistic expectations, investors can mitigate risks and navigate market fluctuations more confidently.

Diversification helps spread risk across different asset classes, while asset allocation balances risk and reward based on individual goals and risk tolerance. Setting realistic investment expectations ensures that investors are prepared for market fluctuations and can make informed decisions aligned with their long-term objectives.

By adhering to these principles and continuously learning and adjusting their strategies, beginner investors can build a solid foundation for successful investing and long-term financial growth.

Chapter 5: What is a Stock Exchange?

Section 1: Definition of a Stock Exchange

Stock exchanges are fundamental components of the financial system, playing a critical role in facilitating the buying and selling of stocks and other securities. This section explores what stock exchanges do, the different types of stock exchanges, and their role in the economy.

What Stock Exchanges Do

1. **Facilitate Trading**
    - **Primary Function:** Stock exchanges provide a regulated platform where buyers and sellers can trade stocks and other securities. They ensure that trades are executed efficiently, transparently, and fairly.
    - **Order Matching:** Exchanges use sophisticated systems to match buy and sell orders. When a buyer and seller agree on a price, the trade is executed according to the exchange's rules and regulations.
    - **Market Liquidity:** Exchanges enhance market liquidity by providing a venue where securities can be bought and sold easily. Higher liquidity reduces the cost of trading and helps ensure fair pricing.
2. **Price Discovery**
    - **Determining Prices:** Stock exchanges play a crucial role in price discovery, which is the process of determining the fair market value of a security. Prices are influenced by supply and demand dynamics and are continuously updated as trades occur.

- **Transparency:** Exchanges provide transparency in pricing by displaying real-time quotes and historical data. This transparency helps investors make informed decisions and fosters confidence in the market.

3. **Regulation and Oversight**

   - **Market Integrity:** Stock exchanges are responsible for enforcing regulations to ensure market integrity and protect investors. They implement rules to prevent fraud, manipulation, and insider trading.
   - **Listing Standards:** Exchanges have stringent listing requirements that companies must meet to be listed. These standards help ensure that only financially sound and reputable companies are available for trading.

Table 1: Functions of Stock Exchanges

Function	Description
Facilitate Trading	Provide a platform for buying and selling securities, ensuring efficient trades.
Price Discovery	Determine the market value of securities through supply and demand.
Regulation and Oversight	Enforce rules to ensure market integrity and protect investors.

Types of Stock Exchanges

1. **Physical Exchanges**

- **Definition:** Physical stock exchanges operate from a physical location where traders meet to execute trades. These exchanges have trading floors where brokers and traders conduct transactions in person.
- **Examples:**
  - **New York Stock Exchange (NYSE):** Located on Wall Street in New York City, the NYSE is one of the largest and most well-known physical exchanges. It operates a trading floor where brokers execute trades through a combination of human and electronic processes.
  - **London Stock Exchange (LSE):** The LSE is one of the oldest stock exchanges in the world, with a trading floor located in London. It provides a platform for trading a wide range of securities.
- **Features:** Physical exchanges are characterized by their trading floors, open outcry systems, and the presence of brokers and traders interacting face-to-face.

Chart 1: Physical Exchange Operations

Note: This is a placeholder. Replace with actual physical exchange chart.

Feature	Description
Trading Floor	Physical location where traders and brokers execute trades.
Open Outcry	Vocal and hand signals used to

Feature	Description
System	communicate buy and sell orders.
Broker Interaction	Brokers facilitate trades on behalf of clients.

2. **Electronic Exchanges**

    - **Definition:** Electronic exchanges operate entirely online, using computerized systems to match buy and sell orders. They eliminate the need for a physical trading floor and rely on technology to facilitate trading.
    - **Examples:**
        - **Nasdaq:** Nasdaq is a prominent electronic exchange known for its technology-focused listings. It operates a fully electronic trading platform and is known for its innovative trading technologies.
        - **BATS Global Markets:** BATS is another electronic exchange that operates in the U.S. and Europe, providing a high-speed, low-latency trading environment.
    - **Features:** Electronic exchanges offer advantages such as faster trade execution, lower costs, and greater accessibility for traders and investors. They use advanced algorithms and automated systems to process trades.

Table 2: Electronic Exchange Features

Feature	Description
Online Platform	Trades are executed electronically through computerized systems.
Speed and Efficiency	Faster trade execution compared to physical exchanges.
Lower Costs	Reduced overhead and transaction costs.

The Role of Exchanges in the Economy

1. **Capital Formation**
    - **Raising Capital:** Stock exchanges facilitate capital formation by allowing companies to raise funds through the issuance of stocks and bonds. Companies can access capital from a broad base of investors, which can be used for expansion, research, and development.
    - **Initial Public Offerings (IPOs):** IPOs enable companies to go public and offer shares to investors for the first time. This process provides companies with access to substantial capital and enhances their visibility and credibility.
2. **Economic Growth**
    - **Investment Opportunities:** Exchanges provide investment opportunities for individuals and institutional investors. By investing in stocks, investors can participate in the growth and success of companies, potentially earning returns on their investments.

- **Market Efficiency:** Exchanges contribute to market efficiency by providing a transparent and regulated environment for trading. Efficient markets allocate resources effectively, contributing to overall economic growth and stability.

3. **Price Discovery and Market Signals**
    - **Reflecting Economic Conditions:** Stock prices on exchanges reflect the collective expectations of investors about the future performance of companies and the overall economy. Changes in stock prices can signal shifts in economic conditions, providing valuable information to policymakers and businesses.
    - **Economic Indicators:** Stock market performance is often used as an indicator of economic health. Rising stock prices may signal economic growth, while declining prices could indicate economic challenges.

Chart 2: Economic Impact of Stock Exchanges

Note: This is a placeholder. Replace with actual economic impact chart.

Role	Description
Capital Formation	Companies raise funds through stock and bond issuance.
Economic Growth	Investment opportunities and efficient resource allocation.
Price Discovery	Reflects economic conditions and provides market signals.

Stock exchanges are essential institutions within the financial system, providing platforms for trading securities, facilitating price discovery, and contributing to economic growth. By understanding the functions and types of stock exchanges, as well as their broader economic role, investors and participants can better appreciate the significance of these markets in facilitating capital formation and reflecting economic conditions.

Physical and electronic exchanges offer different operational models, with physical exchanges relying on in-person interactions and electronic exchanges leveraging technology for faster and more efficient trading. Both types play crucial roles in the financial ecosystem, supporting market liquidity, transparency, and efficiency.

The role of stock exchanges in the economy extends beyond trading; they contribute to capital formation, economic growth, and market efficiency. As investors and market participants, understanding the workings and impact of stock exchanges helps in making informed investment decisions and recognizing the broader economic implications of market activities.

Section 2: Major Global Stock Exchanges

Stock exchanges are pivotal in the global financial system, providing platforms for trading stocks and other securities. This section delves into some of the most prominent stock exchanges around the world, including the New York Stock Exchange (NYSE) and NASDAQ, and explores key international exchanges. It also highlights the differences between major exchanges and their unique characteristics.

1. New York Stock Exchange (NYSE)

Overview:

- **History:** Established in 1792, the New York Stock Exchange (NYSE) is the oldest and largest stock exchange in the world. Its origins trace back to the Buttonwood Agreement signed by 24 stockbrokers on Wall Street.
- **Location:** Located at 11 Wall Street, New York City, the NYSE operates from a historic building known for its iconic façade and bustling trading floor.
- **Market Capitalization:** The NYSE has the highest market capitalization of any stock exchange globally, with listed companies representing a significant portion of the world's total market capitalization.

Key Features:

- **Physical Trading Floor:** The NYSE is known for its physical trading floor where brokers and traders execute transactions. Despite significant automation, the trading floor remains a central feature of the exchange, where trades are conducted through a combination of human interaction and electronic systems.

- **Listed Companies:** The NYSE lists over 2,800 companies, including some of the largest and most well-known corporations such as IBM, Coca-Cola, and General Electric.

- **Market Structure:** The NYSE uses a hybrid trading model combining electronic trading with traditional floor-based trading. This system allows for both high-frequency trading and human intervention.

Table 1: NYSE Overview

Feature	Description
Founded	1792
Location	11 Wall Street, New York City
Market Capitalization	Largest globally
Trading Model	Hybrid (electronic and physical)
Major Listings	IBM, Coca-Cola, General Electric

2. NASDAQ

Overview:

- **History:** Founded in 1971, NASDAQ (National Association of Securities Dealers Automated Quotations) was the world's first electronic stock exchange. It revolutionized trading by offering a fully electronic platform for securities trading.
- **Location:** NASDAQ's operations are based in New York City, but it does not have a physical trading floor. Instead, it operates entirely through electronic systems.

- **Market Capitalization:** NASDAQ is known for its high-tech and growth-oriented companies, including many technology giants.

Key Features:

- **Electronic Trading:** NASDAQ operates as a completely electronic exchange, which allows for faster execution of trades and greater transparency. It uses advanced trading technologies and algorithms to handle high volumes of trades.
- **Listed Companies:** NASDAQ is home to many of the world's largest technology companies, including Apple, Microsoft, and Amazon. It is known for its focus on technology, biotechnology, and emerging growth companies.
- **Market Structure:** NASDAQ operates through a network of market makers who facilitate trading by quoting bid and ask prices. This electronic system enables rapid trading and greater market efficiency.

Table 2: NASDAQ Overview

Feature	Description
Founded	1971
Location	New York City (electronic only)
Market Capitalization	Significant, particularly in technology and growth sectors
Trading Model	Fully electronic
Major Listings	Apple, Microsoft, Amazon

3. Key International Exchanges

1. **London Stock Exchange (LSE)**

    - **Overview:** The London Stock Exchange, established in 1801, is one of the world's oldest stock exchanges. It operates from the City of London and is a major global financial center.
    - **Key Features:**
        - **Listed Companies:** The LSE lists over 2,000 companies from more than 60 countries. It is known for its international reach and diverse range of listed companies.
        - **Market Structure:** The LSE operates both a physical trading floor and an electronic trading platform. It uses a hybrid model similar to the NYSE.
        - **Indices:** The LSE is home to the FTSE 100 Index, which tracks the 100 largest companies listed on the exchange.

    Table 3: LSE Overview

Feature	Description
Founded	1801
Location	London, UK
Market Capitalization	Significant, with a diverse range of international companies
Trading Model	Hybrid (electronic and physical)
Major Listings	BP, HSBC, Unilever

2. **Tokyo Stock Exchange (TSE)**

- **Overview:** The Tokyo Stock Exchange, founded in 1878, is Japan's largest stock exchange and one of the largest in the world by market capitalization.
- **Key Features:**
    - **Listed Companies:** The TSE lists over 3,700 companies, including major Japanese corporations such as Toyota, Sony, and Honda.
    - **Market Structure:** The TSE operates an electronic trading system and is known for its high trading volume and liquidity.
    - **Indices:** The TSE is home to the Nikkei 225 Index, which tracks 225 large, publicly traded companies in Japan.

Table 4: TSE Overview

Feature	Description
Founded	1878
Location	Tokyo, Japan
Market Capitalization	Major global exchange
Trading Model	Electronic
Major Listings	Toyota, Sony, Honda

3. **Hong Kong Stock Exchange (HKEX)**

- **Overview:** Established in 1891, the Hong Kong Stock Exchange is one of Asia's largest and most significant exchanges. It serves as a major gateway for international investors looking to access Chinese markets.

- **Key Features:**
    - **Listed Companies:** The HKEX lists more than 2,500 companies, including major Chinese firms and international companies.
    - **Market Structure:** The HKEX operates an electronic trading system and has a reputation for being a key platform for Chinese companies seeking to raise capital.
    - **Indices:** The HKEX is home to the Hang Seng Index, which tracks the performance of the largest and most liquid companies in Hong Kong.

Table 5: HKEX Overview

Feature	Description
Founded	1891
Location	Hong Kong, China
Market Capitalization	Significant, with a focus on Chinese and international firms
Trading Model	Electronic
Major Listings	Tencent, HSBC, China Mobile

4. **Euronext**

- **Overview:** Euronext is a pan-European stock exchange that was established in 2000. It operates exchanges in Amsterdam, Brussels, Lisbon, and Paris.

- **Key Features:**
  - **Listed Companies:** Euronext lists a diverse range of companies across Europe, including major multinational corporations.
  - **Market Structure:** Euronext operates a fully electronic trading platform and is known for its broad European reach.
  - **Indices:** Euronext is home to the AEX Index, which tracks the performance of the 25 largest Dutch companies.

Table 6: Euronext Overview

Differences Between Major Exchanges

1. **Trading Models**

   - **Physical vs. Electronic:** Exchanges like the NYSE and LSE use a hybrid model combining physical trading floors with electronic systems, whereas NASDAQ, TSE, and HKEX operate fully electronically. This difference affects trading speed, transparency, and the overall trading experience.
   - **Market Makers vs. Specialists:** NASDAQ operates with market makers who provide liquidity by quoting bid and ask prices. In contrast, the NYSE uses specialists who manage specific stocks and facilitate trades.
2. **Market Focus**

- **Sector Focus:** NASDAQ is known for its emphasis on technology and growth companies, while the NYSE lists a broad range of industries, including large blue-chip companies. The TSE and HKEX also have strong representations of technology and industrial companies.
- **International vs. Domestic Listings:** The HKEX and LSE have a strong focus on international and multinational companies, whereas exchanges like the TSE and NYSE have a more domestic focus, although they list numerous international firms.

3. **Regulatory Environment**

   - **Listing Requirements:** Different exchanges have varying listing requirements and regulations. For instance, the NYSE has stringent financial and governance standards, while NASDAQ is known for its focus on emerging growth companies. The TSE has its own set of requirements tailored to Japanese market conditions.
   - **Market Regulation:** Each exchange operates under its own regulatory framework and oversight body, impacting how trading is conducted and how market integrity is maintained.

Table 7: Comparative Analysis of Major Exchanges

Exchange	Trading Model	Market Focus	Regulatory Environment
NYSE	Hybrid	Broad, including	Stringent listing

Exchange	Trading Model	Market Focus	Regulatory Environment
	(physical and electronic)	blue-chip companies	and governance standards
NASDAQ	Fully electronic	Technology and growth companies	Focus on emerging growth companies
TSE	Fully electronic	Diverse, with strong technology and industrial sectors	Tailored to Japanese market conditions
HKEX	Fully electronic	International and Chinese companies	Emphasis on international capital access
Euronext	Fully electronic	European multinational corporations	Broad European regulatory framework

Understanding the major global stock exchanges provides valuable insights into the mechanisms of financial markets and their global impact. Each exchange, from the NYSE and NASDAQ to international platforms like the LSE, TSE, and HKEX, has unique characteristics that influence trading practices, market focus, and regulatory environments.

The NYSE's hybrid trading model combines the tradition of a physical trading floor with modern electronic systems, making it a symbol of historical and contemporary financial practices.

NASDAQ, with its fully electronic platform, represents the cutting edge of trading technology and is a hub for technology and growth-oriented companies.

International exchanges like the LSE, TSE, HKEX, and Euronext play crucial roles in facilitating global investment and capital flows. Each has its own focus and regulatory framework, catering to diverse markets and industries.

By understanding these differences and the specific features of each exchange, investors can make more informed decisions and better navigate the complexities of global financial markets. The global landscape of stock exchanges reflects the dynamic nature of financial markets and the interconnectedness of the world economy.

Section 3: How Exchanges Function

Understanding how stock exchanges function is crucial for grasping the mechanics of financial markets. This section explores the intricacies of order matching, trade execution, the roles of brokers, market makers, and specialists, and the clearing and settlement processes. The section will include graphical representations and tables to provide a clear understanding of these concepts.

1. Order Matching and Trade Execution

Order Matching

Order matching is a fundamental process within a stock exchange that determines how buy and sell orders are paired and executed. Here's how it typically works:

- **Order Types:** Investors can place various types of orders, including market orders (buy/sell immediately at the best available price), limit orders (buy/sell at a specified price or better), and stop orders (trigger a market order when a certain price is reached).
- **Order Book:** Orders are collected in an order book, which is a real-time electronic record of all buy and sell orders for a particular stock. The order book displays order prices, quantities, and the time of order entry.
- **Matching Engine:** The order matching engine is a computerized system that pairs buy and sell orders based on price and time priority. For example, a market buy order will be matched with the lowest available sell order. Limit orders are matched according to their specified prices, and orders with the same price are executed on a first-come, first-served basis.

Trade Execution

Once orders are matched, the trade execution process ensures that transactions are completed efficiently and accurately:

- **Execution Confirmation:** After matching, both buyers and sellers receive confirmation of the trade, including details such as the transaction price, quantity, and trade time.

- **Price Discovery:** The execution process contributes to price discovery, as it reflects the real-time supply and demand dynamics in the market. The price at which a trade is executed becomes the market price for that stock.

- **Speed and Efficiency:** Exchanges use advanced technology to ensure high-speed trade execution. Electronic systems facilitate rapid matching and execution, minimizing latency and enhancing market efficiency.

Table 1: Order Types and Matching

Order Type	Description	Matching Priority
Market Order	Buy/sell immediately at the best available price.	Highest priority
Limit Order	Buy/sell at a specified price or better.	Price and time priority
Stop Order	Trigger a market order when a certain price is reached.	Depends on trigger price

Graph 1: Order Matching Process

Note: This is a placeholder. Replace with actual order matching graph.

2. Role of Brokers, Market Makers, and Specialists

Brokers

Brokers are intermediaries who facilitate trading between buyers and sellers. Their primary functions include:

- **Client Representation:** Brokers represent clients by placing buy or sell orders on their behalf. They provide advice and execute trades according to client instructions.

- **Order Execution:** Brokers execute orders through the exchange's trading system. They may handle both retail and institutional orders, depending on their clientele.
- **Commissions and Fees:** Brokers earn commissions or fees for their services. These costs can vary based on the broker's pricing structure and the type of trade executed.

Table 2: Broker Functions

Function	Description
Client Representation	Place buy/sell orders on behalf of clients.
Order Execution	Execute trades through the exchange.
Commissions and Fees	Earn income from commissions or fees on trades.

Market Makers

Market makers are entities or individuals who provide liquidity to the market by quoting both buy and sell prices for stocks. Their roles include:

- **Providing Liquidity:** Market makers ensure that there is always a buyer or seller for a stock, enhancing market liquidity and reducing bid-ask spreads.
- **Quote Management:** They continuously update bid and ask prices based on market conditions and their inventory of stocks.
- **Profit from Spread:** Market makers profit from the difference between the bid price (buy) and the ask price

(sell). This spread compensates them for providing liquidity and taking on the risk of holding inventory.

Table 3: Market Maker Functions

Function	Description
Providing Liquidity	Ensure there is a buyer or seller for stocks.
Quote Management	Update bid and ask prices continuously.
Profit from Spread	Earn from the difference between bid and ask prices.

Specialists

Specialists, also known as Designated Market Makers (DMMs) on the NYSE, play a unique role in facilitating trading:

- **Managing Specific Stocks:** Specialists are assigned specific stocks and are responsible for maintaining a fair and orderly market for those stocks.
- **Order Execution:** They handle buy and sell orders for their assigned stocks, ensuring that trades are executed smoothly and that the market for those stocks remains liquid.
- **Price Stabilization:** Specialists help stabilize prices by managing large orders and intervening when necessary to prevent excessive volatility.

Table 4: Specialist Functions

3. Clearing and Settlement Processes

Clearing

Clearing is the process of confirming and reconciling trades to ensure that both parties meet their obligations:

- **Trade Confirmation:** After a trade is executed, the clearing process involves confirming the trade details between the buyer and seller. This includes verifying the transaction price, quantity, and other relevant information.
- **Clearing Houses:** Clearing houses, such as the Depository Trust & Clearing Corporation (DTCC) in the U.S., act as intermediaries between buyers and sellers. They facilitate the clearing process and manage the risk associated with trade settlement.
- **Netting:** Clearing houses perform netting, which involves offsetting buy and sell positions to determine the net obligations of each party. This reduces the total number of transactions and simplifies the settlement process.

Table 5: Clearing Process

Step	Description
Trade Confirmation	Verify trade details between buyer and seller.
Clearing Houses	Act as intermediaries to facilitate trade reconciliation.
Netting	Offset buy and sell positions to simplify

Step	Description
	settlement.

Settlement

Settlement is the process of transferring ownership of securities and funds between parties:

- **Settlement Date:** The settlement date is the date by which the buyer must pay for the securities and the seller must deliver the securities. The standard settlement period for most stocks is T+2 (trade date plus two business days).
- **Delivery vs. Payment:** Settlement involves two key components: delivery (transfer of securities) and payment (transfer of funds). The securities and funds are exchanged simultaneously to ensure that both parties fulfill their obligations.
- **Settlement Systems:** Exchanges and clearing houses use electronic systems to facilitate the settlement process, reducing the risk of errors and delays. These systems ensure that transactions are completed efficiently and accurately.

Table 6: Settlement Process

Step	Description
Settlement Date	Date by which payment and delivery must be completed (T+2).
Delivery vs. Payment	Transfer of securities and funds simultaneously.

Step	Description
Settlement Systems	Use electronic systems to ensure accurate and efficient settlements.

Graph 2: Clearing and Settlement Process

Note: This is a placeholder. Replace with actual clearing and settlement graph.

Stock exchanges are complex institutions with multifaceted functions that ensure the smooth operation of financial markets. The processes of order matching, trade execution, and clearing and settlement are critical for maintaining market efficiency, transparency, and integrity.

Order matching involves sophisticated systems that pair buy and sell orders based on price and time priorities. The roles of brokers, market makers, and specialists are essential in providing liquidity, executing trades, and managing specific stocks, each contributing to the overall functionality of the market.

Clearing and settlement processes further ensure that trades are confirmed, reconciled, and settled accurately. These processes, facilitated by clearing houses and electronic systems, are crucial for minimizing risk and ensuring that transactions are completed seamlessly.

Understanding these functions and processes provides valuable insights into how stock exchanges operate and maintain their crucial role in the global financial system. By appreciating the intricacies of these mechanisms, investors and market participants can better navigate the complexities of financial markets and make more informed decisions.

Chapter 6: The Role of Market Capitalization

Section 1: Understanding Market Capitalization

Market capitalization, or market cap, is a fundamental metric used to assess the size and value of a company in the financial markets. This section provides a detailed examination of market capitalization, including its definition, calculation methods, categories, and its significance in investment decisions. Graphical representations, data tables, and diagrams will be used to enhance understanding.

1. Definition and Calculation

Definition:

Market capitalization is the total market value of a company's outstanding shares of stock. It provides a snapshot of a company's overall value as perceived by the market and is used to categorize companies into various size segments. Market cap is a key indicator of a company's size, stability, and growth potential.

Calculation:

The calculation of market capitalization is straightforward. It is determined by multiplying the current stock price by the total number of outstanding shares:

Market Capitalization=Stock Price×Outstanding Shares\text{Market Capitalization} = \text{Stock Price} \times \text{Outstanding Shares}Market Capitalization=Stock Price×Outstanding Shares

Example Calculation:

If a company has 1,000,000 shares outstanding and the current stock price is \$50, the market capitalization would be:

Market Capitalization=1,000,000×50=\$50,000,000\text{Market Capitalization} = 1,000,000 \times 50 = \\$50,000,000Market Capitalization=1,000,000×50=\$50,000,000

Table 1: Market Capitalization Calculation Example

Parameter	Value
Outstanding Shares	1,000,000
Stock Price	\$50
Market	**\$50,000,00**

Parameter	Value
Capitalization	0

Diagram 1: Market Capitalization Calculation

Note: This is a placeholder. Replace with an actual diagram illustrating the calculation.

2. Market Cap Categories

Market capitalization is often categorized into different segments to better understand a company's size and its relative position within the market. The main categories are:

a. Micro Cap

- **Definition:** Micro cap stocks are companies with a market capitalization typically under $300 million. These companies are often in the early stages of development and may have limited financial resources.
- **Characteristics:** High growth potential, but also higher risk and volatility. Micro cap stocks can be subject to greater market fluctuations and less liquidity.
- **Examples:** Startups, small technology firms, and early-stage ventures.

b. Small Cap

- **Definition:** Small cap stocks have market capitalizations ranging from $300 million to $2 billion. These companies are generally more established than micro caps but still have significant growth potential.

- **Characteristics:** Higher growth potential compared to larger companies, but also higher risk compared to mid and large cap stocks. They may offer substantial investment opportunities.
- **Examples:** Regional banks, emerging consumer brands, and specialized manufacturers.

c. Mid Cap

- **Definition:** Mid cap stocks have market capitalizations between $2 billion and $10 billion. These companies are often well-established with a strong market presence.
- **Characteristics:** Balances growth potential and stability. Mid cap stocks can offer good growth prospects while being less volatile than small caps.
- **Examples:** Established technology firms, mid-sized industrial companies, and consumer goods companies.

d. Large Cap

- **Definition:** Large cap stocks are companies with market capitalizations exceeding $10 billion. These companies are typically industry leaders with a strong market position.
- **Characteristics:** Generally more stable and less volatile than smaller cap stocks. They often provide steady dividends and are considered safer investments.
- **Examples:** Major technology companies, large multinational corporations, and blue-chip stocks.

e. Mega Cap

- **Definition:** Mega cap stocks represent the largest companies with market capitalizations over $200 billion. They are global leaders in their respective industries.
- **Characteristics:** Very stable and low volatility. Mega caps often dominate their sectors and have substantial global influence.
- **Examples:** Tech giants like Apple, Microsoft, and Amazon.

Table 2: Market Cap Categories

Category	Market Cap Range	Characteristics	Examples
Micro Cap	Under $300M	High risk and volatility; high growth potential	Startups, small tech firms
Small Cap	$300M - $2B	Higher growth potential; moderate risk	Regional banks, emerging brands
Mid Cap	$2B - $10B	Balanced growth and stability	Established tech firms, mid-sized companies
Large Cap	Over $10B	Stable, lower volatility; often blue-chip	Major tech companies, multinational corporations
Mega Cap	Over $200B	Very stable, global leaders	Apple, Microsoft, Amazon

Diagram 2: Market Cap Categories

Note: This is a placeholder. Replace with an actual diagram showing market cap categories.

3. Why Market Cap Matters

a. Investment Decisions

Market capitalization is crucial for making investment decisions. It helps investors:

- **Assess Risk and Return:** Different market cap categories have varying risk and return profiles. Small and micro cap stocks generally offer higher growth potential but come with greater risk, while large and mega cap stocks provide stability and often pay dividends.
- **Diversify Portfolios:** Understanding market cap allows investors to diversify their portfolios across different categories, balancing high-risk, high-reward investments with more stable, lower-risk options.

b. Company Evaluation

Market cap provides insights into a company's relative size and market position:

- **Size and Influence:** Large and mega cap companies are often industry leaders with significant market influence. Their size can indicate financial stability, strong revenue generation, and established market presence.
- **Growth Potential:** Smaller cap stocks may offer higher growth potential, especially if they are in emerging

industries or innovative sectors. However, they also come with higher uncertainty and volatility.

c. Market Trends and Indices

Market capitalization plays a role in market trends and index composition:

- **Market Indices:** Many market indices, such as the S&P 500 and NASDAQ-100, are weighted by market cap. This means that companies with larger market capitalizations have a greater impact on the index's performance.
- **Economic Indicators:** The performance of different market cap segments can serve as indicators of broader economic trends. For example, strong performance in small cap stocks may suggest investor optimism about economic growth, while large cap performance might indicate stability.

Table 3: Market Cap and Investment Strategies

Investment Strategy	Market Cap Focus	Pros	Cons
Growth Investing	Small Cap, Micro Cap	High growth potential, potential for high returns	Higher risk and volatility
Value Investing	Mid Cap, Large Cap	Balanced risk and growth, often stable	Lower growth compared to small caps

Investment Strategy	Market Cap Focus	Pros	Cons
Income Investing	Large Cap, Mega Cap	Stable dividends, lower risk	Lower growth potential
Diversification	Across Market Caps	Balances risk and returns	Requires careful selection and management

Diagram 3: Impact of Market Cap on Investment Strategies

Note: This is a placeholder. Replace with an actual diagram illustrating how market cap impacts investment strategies.

Market capitalization is a key metric that provides valuable insights into a company's size, market position, and potential for growth. By understanding the definition, calculation, categories, and significance of market cap, investors can make more informed decisions and develop strategies that align with their investment goals.

The various market cap categories—micro cap, small cap, mid cap, large cap, and mega cap—each offer distinct characteristics and investment opportunities. Whether seeking high growth, stability, or income, market cap helps investors assess risk, diversify portfolios, and evaluate companies effectively.

The role of market capitalization extends beyond individual investment decisions to influencing market trends and index performance. By analyzing market cap data and trends, investors can gain a comprehensive understanding of the market landscape and make strategic investment choices.

Understanding these concepts, supported by graphical representations and data tables, provides a clear perspective on the importance of market capitalization in the financial markets.

Section 2: Categories: Micro, Small, Mid, Large, and Mega Cap Stocks

Market capitalization (market cap) is a crucial metric used to categorize companies based on their total market value, derived from their stock price multiplied by the number of outstanding shares. Understanding the characteristics, risks, and opportunities associated with each market cap category—Micro, Small, Mid, Large, and Mega Cap—can help investors make informed decisions and tailor their investment strategies effectively. This section delves into the specific attributes of each market cap category, the associated risks and opportunities, and how investors can leverage this knowledge to craft their investment approach.

1. Characteristics of Each Market Cap Category

Micro Cap Stocks

- **Definition:** Micro cap stocks are companies with a market capitalization typically under $300 million. These companies are often in the early stages of development or operate in niche markets.

- **Characteristics:**
    - **High Growth Potential:** Micro cap stocks may offer significant growth potential due to their early stage of development and innovative business models.
    - **Limited Resources:** These companies may have limited financial resources, which can impact their ability to scale operations or weather economic downturns.
    - **Less Established:** They are often less established than larger companies and may lack a proven track record.

Small Cap Stocks

- **Definition:** Small cap stocks have market capitalizations ranging from $300 million to $2 billion. These companies are typically more established than micro caps but are still growing.
- **Characteristics:**
    - **Growth Opportunities:** Small cap stocks often have substantial growth opportunities and can offer attractive returns as they expand their market presence.
    - **Moderate Risk:** While generally riskier than mid and large cap stocks, they are less volatile than micro caps and may provide a balance between growth and stability.

    - **Innovation:** Many small cap companies are involved in innovative sectors or emerging industries.

Mid Cap Stocks

- **Definition:** Mid cap stocks have market capitalizations between $2 billion and $10 billion. These companies are usually well-established and have a solid market position.
- **Characteristics:**
    - **Balanced Growth:** Mid cap stocks offer a blend of growth potential and stability. They are often seen as having more growth potential than large caps but are less risky than small caps.
    - **Established Market Presence:** They typically have a more substantial market presence and a more diversified revenue stream compared to small caps.
    - **Moderate Volatility:** Mid cap stocks experience moderate volatility, offering a balance of risk and return.

Large Cap Stocks

- **Definition:** Large cap stocks are companies with market capitalizations exceeding $10 billion. These companies are usually industry leaders with a strong market position.
- **Characteristics:**

    - **Stability:** Large cap stocks are generally more stable and less volatile. They often have established business models and diversified operations.
    - **Steady Returns:** They typically provide steady returns and may pay regular dividends, making them appealing to conservative investors.
    - **Global Influence:** Many large cap companies have a global presence and substantial influence in their industries.

Mega Cap Stocks

- **Definition:** Mega cap stocks represent the largest companies, with market capitalizations over $200 billion. These companies are often dominant players in their respective industries.
- **Characteristics:**
    - **Extensive Market Influence:** Mega caps wield significant market influence and often have substantial resources and global reach.
    - **Low Volatility:** They tend to be very stable, with low volatility due to their size and established market position.
    - **Blue-Chip Status:** Mega cap stocks are often considered blue-chip, representing high-quality companies with strong financials and a long history of performance.

Table 1: Characteristics of Market Cap Categories

Market Cap Category	Market Cap Range	Characteristics
Micro Cap	Under $300M	High growth potential, limited resources, less established
Small Cap	$300M - $2B	Substantial growth opportunities, moderate risk, innovative sectors
Mid Cap	$2B - $10B	Balanced growth and stability, established market presence
Large Cap	Over $10B	Stability, steady returns, global influence
Mega Cap	Over $200B	Extensive market influence, low volatility, blue-chip status

Diagram 1: Market Cap Categories

Note: This is a placeholder. Replace with an actual diagram illustrating the market cap categories.

2. Risks and Opportunities in Each Segment

Micro Cap Stocks

- **Risks:**
    - **High Volatility:** Micro cap stocks can be extremely volatile, with significant price swings that may be influenced by market sentiment and speculative trading.
    - **Limited Liquidity:** These stocks may have lower trading volumes, leading to wider bid-ask spreads

and difficulty executing large trades without impacting the stock price.

- **Higher Failure Rate:** Micro cap companies may face a higher risk of business failure due to limited resources and less financial stability.

- **Opportunities:**
    - **High Growth Potential:** Micro cap stocks can experience rapid growth and significant appreciation if the company succeeds in its business endeavors.
    - **Undervalued Assets:** Investors may find undervalued stocks with strong growth potential that are overlooked by larger market participants.

Small Cap Stocks

- **Risks:**
    - **Moderate Volatility:** While less volatile than micro caps, small cap stocks still experience fluctuations that can impact investment returns.
    - **Business Risks:** Small cap companies may face operational challenges, including competition and market changes, which can affect profitability and stock performance.
- **Opportunities:**
    - **Growth Prospects:** Small cap stocks often offer substantial growth potential as they expand their operations and gain market share.

- **Innovation:** Many small cap companies are involved in emerging industries or innovative technologies, providing opportunities for high returns.

Mid Cap Stocks

- **Risks:**
    - **Economic Sensitivity:** Mid cap stocks can be sensitive to economic cycles, experiencing fluctuations in performance based on broader economic conditions.
    - **Competitive Pressures:** They may face intense competition from both smaller and larger companies, impacting their growth and profitability.
- **Opportunities:**
    - **Balanced Growth and Stability:** Mid cap stocks offer a blend of growth and stability, making them suitable for investors seeking a balanced approach.
    - **Expansion Potential:** These companies often have established business models and are well-positioned for expansion and increased market share.

Large Cap Stocks

- **Risks:**
    - **Market Saturation:** Large cap companies may face challenges related to market saturation and

slower growth rates compared to smaller companies.

  - **Regulatory and Political Risks:** They can be impacted by regulatory changes and political events that affect their global operations and profitability.
- **Opportunities:**
  - **Steady Returns:** Large cap stocks provide stability and often pay dividends, making them attractive to income-focused investors.
  - **Global Reach:** These companies have extensive market reach and established market positions, providing opportunities for steady growth and profitability.

Mega Cap Stocks

- **Risks:**
  - **Limited Upside Potential:** Due to their size and market dominance, mega cap stocks may experience slower growth compared to smaller companies.
  - **Regulatory Scrutiny:** They may face increased regulatory scrutiny and potential challenges related to market dominance and anti-trust issues.
- **Opportunities:**
  - **Low Volatility:** Mega cap stocks offer stability and low volatility, making them suitable for conservative investors seeking reliable returns.

- **Strong Financials:** These companies often have robust financials and significant resources, allowing them to navigate economic downturns effectively.

Table 2: Risks and Opportunities by Market Cap Category

Market Cap Category	Risks	Opportunities
Micro Cap	High volatility, limited liquidity, higher failure rate	High growth potential, undervalued assets
Small Cap	Moderate volatility, business risks	Growth prospects, innovation
Mid Cap	Economic sensitivity, competitive pressures	Balanced growth and stability, expansion potential
Large Cap	Market saturation, regulatory and political risks	Steady returns, global reach
Mega Cap	Limited upside potential, regulatory scrutiny	Low volatility, strong financials

Diagram 2: Risk vs. Opportunity by Market Cap Category

Note: This is a placeholder. Replace with an actual

diagram showing the risk vs. opportunity for each market cap category.

3. How to Invest Based on Market Cap

Investing based on market cap requires understanding the characteristics and risk profiles of different categories and aligning them with investment goals. Here's how to approach investing in each market cap segment:

Micro Cap Stocks

- **Investment Strategy:**
  - **High Risk Tolerance:** Investors in micro caps should have a high risk tolerance and be prepared for significant price volatility.
  - **Due Diligence:** Conduct thorough research and due diligence to identify promising micro cap opportunities with strong growth potential.
  - **Diversification:** Diversify investments across multiple micro cap stocks to mitigate risk and increase the likelihood of capturing high-growth opportunities.

Small Cap Stocks

- **Investment Strategy:**
  - **Growth Focus:** Focus on companies with strong growth prospects and innovative business models.
  - **Research and Analysis:** Perform detailed analysis of financial health, market position, and growth potential to select attractive small cap stocks.

- **Monitor Performance:** Regularly monitor the performance of small cap investments and stay informed about market trends and economic conditions that may impact these stocks.

Mid Cap Stocks

- **Investment Strategy:**
  - **Balanced Approach:** Invest in mid cap stocks for a balance of growth and stability. They offer a good mix of potential returns and moderate risk.
  - **Evaluate Market Position:** Assess the company's market position, financial performance, and growth prospects to identify attractive mid cap stocks.
  - **Long-Term Investment:** Consider mid cap stocks for long-term investment strategies, as they often provide steady growth and stability over time.

Large Cap Stocks

- **Investment Strategy:**
  - **Stability and Income:** Large cap stocks are suitable for investors seeking stability and income, often through dividends.
  - **Blue-Chip Focus:** Invest in blue-chip large cap companies with a strong track record and established market presence.
  - **Economic Conditions:** Consider economic conditions and market trends that may impact large

cap stocks, and adjust investment strategies accordingly.

Mega Cap Stocks

- **Investment Strategy:**
    - **Conservative Approach:** Mega cap stocks are ideal for conservative investors seeking low volatility and reliable returns.
    - **Global Diversification:** Leverage the global presence and market influence of mega cap companies to benefit from their established position in the market.
    - **Long-Term Holdings:** Invest in mega cap stocks as long-term holdings to benefit from their stability and strong financials.

Table 3: Investment Strategies by Market Cap Category

Market Cap Category	Investment Strategy	Considerations
Micro Cap	High risk tolerance, due diligence, diversification	Significant volatility, high growth potential
Small Cap	Growth focus, research and analysis, performance monitoring	Moderate volatility, innovative sectors
Mid Cap	Balanced approach,	Growth and

Market Cap Category	Investment Strategy	Considerations
	evaluate market position, long-term investment	stability balance
Large Cap	Stability and income, blue-chip focus, economic conditions	Reliable returns, steady dividends
Mega Cap	Conservative approach, global diversification, long-term holdings	Low volatility, strong financials

Diagram 3: Investment Strategy by Market Cap

Note: This is a placeholder. Replace with an actual diagram illustrating investment strategies for each market cap category.

Understanding the characteristics, risks, and opportunities associated with each market cap category—Micro, Small, Mid, Large, and Mega Cap—is essential for making informed investment decisions. Each category offers unique attributes that cater to different investment goals and risk tolerances. By aligning investment strategies with market cap segments, investors can optimize their portfolios and achieve their financial objectives.

Investors should carefully evaluate each market cap category, considering factors such as volatility, growth potential, and stability. Diversification across various market cap segments can help manage risk and enhance overall portfolio performance. By leveraging the insights provided in this section, investors can develop a well-rounded investment approach that aligns with their individual goals and preferences.

Section 3: Market Cap vs. Company Valuation

In the realm of investing, market capitalization (market cap) and company valuation are fundamental concepts that investors use to assess the worth of a company. While market cap provides a straightforward measure of a company's size, it does not encompass the full picture of a company's financial health and value. Understanding the distinctions between market cap and enterprise value, how market cap reflects a company's size and growth potential, and addressing common misconceptions can significantly enhance investment decision-making. This section explores these aspects in detail, supported by diagrams, data, and graphs.

1. Market Cap vs. Enterprise Value

Market Cap:

- **Definition:** Market capitalization, or market cap, is calculated by multiplying a company's current stock price by its total number of outstanding shares. This metric provides an estimate of the company's total equity value as perceived by the stock market. The formula is:

Market Capitalization=Stock Price×Outstanding Shares\text{Market Capitalization} = \text{Stock Price} \times \text{Outstanding Shares}Market Capitalization=Stock Price×Outstanding Shares

- **Purpose:** Market cap is widely used to categorize companies into different size categories (e.g., micro, small, mid, large, and mega cap). It provides a snapshot of a company's size and is a useful indicator for comparing companies within the same industry.
- **Limitations:** While market cap reflects the equity value of a company, it does not account for the company's debt or cash reserves. This limitation means that market cap alone does not provide a comprehensive view of a company's total value.

Enterprise Value (EV):

- **Definition:** Enterprise value is a more comprehensive measure that reflects the total value of a company, including its debt and cash reserves. It is calculated using the formula:

  Enterprise Value=Market Capitalization+Total Debt−Cash and Cash Equivalents\text{Enterprise Value} = \text{Market Capitalization} + \text{Total Debt} - \text{Cash and Cash Equivalents}Enterprise Value=Market Capitalization+Total Debt−Cash and Cash Equivalents

- **Purpose:** EV is used to assess a company's total value, especially in the context of mergers and acquisitions. It represents the theoretical cost to acquire a company, considering both its equity and debt.
- **Advantages:** EV provides a more complete picture of a company's value by including debt and cash reserves, offering insights into the company's financial health and capital structure.

Table 1: Market Cap vs. Enterprise Value

Metric	Market Cap	Enterprise Value
Definition	Equity value based on stock price	Total value including debt and cash
Formula	Stock Price × Outstanding Shares	Market Cap + Total Debt - Cash and Cash Equivalents
Focus	Reflects equity value	Reflects total company value
Use Case	Stock market analysis, size categorization	Acquisition valuation, debt considerations

Diagram 1: Market Cap vs. Enterprise Value

Note: This is a placeholder. Replace with an actual diagram illustrating the difference between market cap and enterprise value.

2. How Market Cap Reflects Company Size and Growth Potential

Reflecting Company Size:

- **Size Classification:** Market cap categorizes companies into different size brackets: micro, small, mid, large, and mega cap. These classifications help investors understand the relative size of a company compared to its peers. For instance:
    - **Micro Cap:** Companies with market caps under $300 million, often in the early stages or niche markets.
    - **Small Cap:** Companies with market caps between $300 million and $2 billion, typically growing and more established than micro caps.
    - **Mid Cap:** Companies with market caps between $2 billion and $10 billion, well-established with solid market positions.
    - **Large Cap:** Companies with market caps over $10 billion, major players in their industries.
    - **Mega Cap:** Companies with market caps over $200 billion, dominant players with significant global influence.
- **Market Perception:** A higher market cap generally indicates a larger, more established company with a significant market presence. Conversely, a lower market cap suggests a smaller, potentially less stable company. Market cap provides a quick gauge of a company's size, but it does not reflect all aspects of its financial health.

Reflecting Growth Potential:

- **Growth Expectations:** Market cap can indicate a company's growth stage and potential. Generally:
  - **Micro and Small Cap Stocks:** Often have high growth potential due to their smaller size and earlier stage of development. These stocks may offer substantial returns if the company grows rapidly.
  - **Mid Cap Stocks:** Typically represent companies that have outgrown their small cap phase and are positioned for continued growth. They offer a balance between risk and return.
  - **Large and Mega Cap Stocks:** Usually have slower growth rates due to their established market presence and maturity. However, they tend to be more stable and provide consistent returns.
- **Investment Risk:** Higher market cap companies are often seen as less risky due to their established market positions and financial stability. Smaller market cap companies may offer higher growth potential but come with greater risk and volatility. Investors need to balance their risk tolerance with potential returns when considering market cap.

Table 2: Market Cap and Growth Potential

Market Cap Category	Size Reflection	Growth Potential
Micro Cap	Smallest size, often emerging or niche markets	High growth potential, high risk

Market Cap Category	Size Reflection	Growth Potential
Small Cap	Growing companies, moderate size	Significant growth opportunities, moderate risk
Mid Cap	Established, mid-sized companies	Balanced growth, moderate stability
Large Cap	Major industry players, large size	Stable growth, lower growth potential
Mega Cap	Largest companies, dominant market presence	Stable growth, limited growth potential

Diagram 2: Market Cap and Company Size

Note: This is a placeholder. Replace with an actual diagram illustrating the relationship between market cap and company size.

3. Misconceptions About Market Cap

Misconception 1: Market Cap Equals Company Value

- **Clarification:** Market cap only reflects the value of a company's equity and does not account for its debt or cash reserves. This limitation means that market cap alone may not provide a complete view of a company's total value.
- **Example:** Consider two companies with identical market caps. One company may have substantial debt, while the other has significant cash reserves. The enterprise value

of these companies would differ, revealing different financial realities beyond market cap.

Misconception 2: Market Cap Determines Financial Health

- **Clarification:** Market cap does not provide insights into a company's financial health, such as its debt levels, cash flow, or profitability. These factors are critical for assessing the overall stability and performance of a company.
- **Example:** A company with a large market cap might still face financial difficulties if it has high levels of debt or declining revenues. Conversely, a smaller company with strong financial metrics might be undervalued by the market.

Misconception 3: High Market Cap Guarantees Future Success

- **Clarification:** A high market cap indicates current market valuation but does not guarantee future performance or success. Factors such as market conditions, industry trends, and company performance play a significant role in determining future outcomes.
- **Example:** A large tech company with a high market cap may face challenges such as technological disruption or regulatory issues that could impact its future growth and profitability.

Table 3: Common Misconceptions About Market Cap

Misconception	Clarification	Implications
Market Cap Equals Company Value	Market cap only reflects equity value, not total value	Misleading when evaluating total company value
Market Cap Determines Financial Health	Market cap does not account for debt or cash reserves	Financial health requires a comprehensive analysis
High Market Cap Guarantees Future Success	Market cap does not guarantee future performance	Future success depends on multiple factors

Diagram 3: Market Cap vs. Company Value

Note: This is a placeholder. Replace with an actual diagram illustrating market cap compared to total company value.

Market capitalization provides a valuable measure of a company's size and market perception, but it is only one piece of the puzzle when evaluating a company's overall value. By understanding the differences between market cap and enterprise value, investors can gain a more comprehensive view of a company's financial standing. While market cap reflects equity value and company size, enterprise value offers a fuller picture by incorporating debt and cash reserves.

Recognizing how market cap reflects company size and growth potential is crucial for aligning investment strategies with risk tolerance and return expectations. Additionally, addressing common misconceptions about market cap helps investors make more informed decisions and avoid pitfalls associated with relying solely on market cap for valuation purposes.

Incorporating these insights into investment analysis, supported by detailed tables, diagrams, and data, equips investors with a robust understanding of market capitalization and its role in company valuation. This knowledge enables more accurate assessments of investment opportunities and better decision-making in the financial markets.

Chapter 7: Common Stock Investing Mistakes to Avoid

Investing in stocks can be rewarding, but many investors fall into common traps that hinder their success. This chapter aims to identify these mistakes, explain their consequences, and offer practical strategies to avoid them. Understanding these pitfalls can lead to better decision-making and improved long-term performance.

Section 1: Unrealistic Expectations and Goal Setting

One of the most common mistakes in stock investing is setting unrealistic expectations and failing to establish clear, attainable goals. This section addresses why this happens and how to set realistic expectations and investment goals.

1.1 Expecting Unrealistic Returns or Relying on Others' Expectations

Many investors enter the stock market with high hopes of achieving outsized returns, often based on hype, social media influencers, or unrealistic comparisons.

1. **Understanding Reasonable Rate of Return**
    - **Historical Returns**: Over the long term, the S&P 500 has averaged an annual return of around 7-10% adjusted for inflation.
    - **Unrealistic Expectations**: New investors often expect returns of 20-30% annually, which is unsustainable without significant risk.
2. **Developing Your Own Investment Goals**
    - **Personalized Goals**: Tailor goals based on your financial situation, risk tolerance, and time horizon rather than following the crowd.
    - **SMART Goals**: Specific, Measurable, Achievable, Relevant, and Time-bound objectives can help set realistic expectations.

3. **Avoiding Performance Hype**
    - **Media Influence**: Be wary of media hype around "hot stocks" or investment fads, as these can skew expectations and lead to impulsive decisions.
    - **Reality Check**: Use financial models and historical data to ground your expectations in reality.

Chart 1: Expected vs. Realistic Stock Market Returns
A bar chart comparing unrealistic investor expectations (20-30%) versus historical average returns (7-10%) over various periods.

1.2 Neglecting to Set Clear Investment Goals

Failing to define clear investment goals often leads to unstructured decision-making and suboptimal outcomes.

1. **Importance of Defining Clear Objectives**
    - **Financial Milestones**: Goals such as retirement savings, buying a home, or funding education should guide your investment strategy.
    - **Risk and Time Alignment**: Goals should align with your risk tolerance and investment time horizon.
2. **Risks of Over-Concentration in Single Stock or Sector**
    - **Example**: Investors focused heavily on tech stocks in the 2000s suffered significant losses during the dot-com crash.

- **Diversification**: Clear goals help prevent over-concentration in single assets or sectors.

3. **Aligning Goals with Investment Strategy**

   - **Growth vs. Income**: Decide if you're seeking capital appreciation or steady income and align your portfolio accordingly.
   - **Rebalancing**: Regularly review and adjust your portfolio to ensure it remains aligned with your objectives.

List: Tips for Setting Clear Investment Goals

- Break down goals by timeline: short-term, medium-term, long-term.
- Regularly review and adjust goals as your life circumstances change.
- Document your investment strategy and rationale for each goal.

1.3 Failing to Adequately Diversify Your Portfolio

Diversification is a critical risk management strategy that many investors neglect, leading to unnecessary exposure to market volatility.

1. **Risks of Lack of Diversification**

   - **Concentrated Risk**: Holding too many stocks from one sector increases vulnerability to sector-specific downturns.

- **Example**: The collapse of Enron affected investors who held a significant portion of their portfolio in the stock.

2. **Importance of Sector and Asset Diversification**
    - **Sector Diversification**: Spreading investments across different industries reduces risk.
    - **Asset Classes**: Include stocks, bonds, real estate, and other assets to balance risk and reward.
3. **Strategies for Effective Diversification**
    - **Use of ETFs and Mutual Funds**: These funds provide built-in diversification across a broad range of stocks and sectors.
    - **Global Exposure**: Invest in international stocks to diversify beyond domestic markets.

Table 1: Diversification Impact on Portfolio Risk

Portfolio Type	Number of Stocks	Sector Exposure	Risk Level	Historical Return (%)
Concentrated Portfolio	5	Single Sector	High	12%
Diversified Portfolio	20	Multi-Sector	Medium	8%
Balanced Asset Mix	30+	Multi-Sector	Low	10%

Section 2: Trading Errors and High Costs

Many investors lose money due to poor trading decisions and high costs associated with frequent trading and advisory fees.

This section explores common trading errors and how to minimize them.

2.1 Buying High and Selling Low

The most classic mistake in stock investing is panic selling during market dips and buying during peaks, driven by emotional decision-making.

1. **Understanding Market Cycles and Trends**
    - **Bull vs. Bear Markets**: Recognize that markets move in cycles; bull markets are characterized by rising prices, while bear markets are downturns.
    - **Emotional Investing**: Avoid letting fear or greed dictate buy and sell decisions.
2. **Strategies for Avoiding Common Trading Errors**
    - **Dollar-Cost Averaging**: Invest a fixed amount regularly, which mitigates the impact of market volatility.
    - **Set Limit Orders**: Use stop-loss and take-profit orders to automate decisions and remove emotion.
3. **Impact on Long-Term Returns**
    - **Missed Opportunities**: Selling during downturns locks in losses, while missing market rebounds can severely impact returns.
    - **Patience is Key**: Historical data shows that long-term investors often outperform those who frequently trade.

Chart 2: Buy High, Sell Low - Impact on Returns

A line graph showing the negative impact of buying high and selling low on portfolio growth over time.

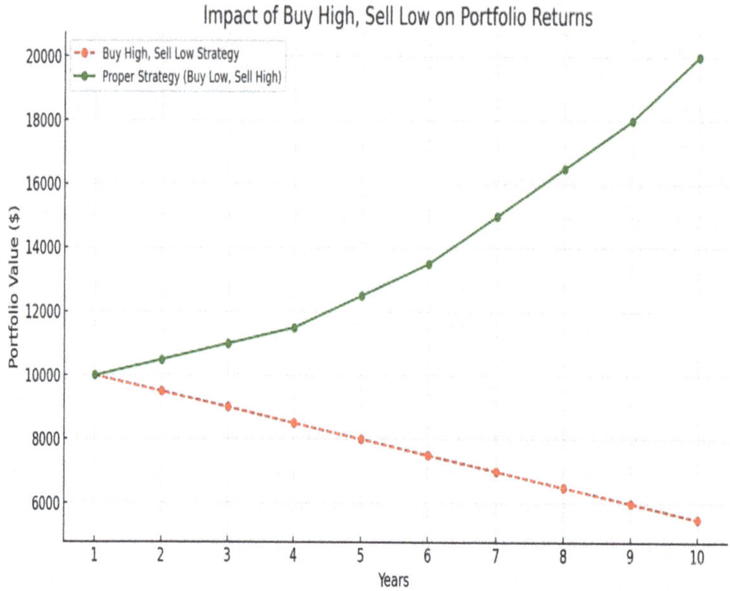

The chart above illustrates the negative impact of a "Buy High, Sell Low" strategy on portfolio growth compared to a more disciplined approach of "Buy Low, Sell High."

2.2 Trading Too Frequently and Incurring High Fees

Frequent trading often leads to high costs, which can eat into profits and negatively impact overall returns.

1. **Overpaying in Fees and Commissions**

    - **Cost Analysis**: Frequent trades generate transaction fees that add up over time, reducing overall returns.

- **Commission-Free Platforms**: Use platforms offering commission-free trades to minimize costs.

2. **Impact of High Fees on Long-Term Returns**
    - **Compounding Costs**: A seemingly small fee can significantly affect returns when compounded over time.
    - **Illustration**: A 1% fee on a $100,000 portfolio over 30 years could cost over $76,000 in potential returns.
3. **Balancing Trading Frequency and Costs**
    - **Long-Term Strategies**: Focus on long-term investment rather than short-term gains to reduce trading costs.
    - **Portfolio Turnover**: Keep turnover low to minimize costs and improve net returns.

Table 2: The Cost of Frequent Trading

Number of Trades Per Year	Average Commission per Trade	Annual Cost	10-Year Cost	30-Year Cost
10	$10	$100	$1,000	$3,000
50	$10	$500	$5,000	$15,000
100	$10	$1,000	$10,000	$30,000

2.3 Seeking Value in Advisory Fees

While professional advice can be valuable, investors must weigh the benefits against the costs associated with advisory services.

1. **Evaluating the Value of Advisory Services**
    - **Fee Models**: Advisors charge flat fees, hourly rates, or a percentage of assets under management (AUM).
    - **Benefits**: Access to professional guidance, personalized portfolio management, and strategic planning.
2. **Balancing Costs with Benefits**
    - **Cost-Benefit Analysis**: Consider if the performance improvements justify the fees. For some, a DIY approach using low-cost index funds may be more cost-effective.
    - **Low-Cost Alternatives**: Robo-advisors and online tools can provide guidance at a fraction of the cost.
3. **Understanding the Impact of Fees on Investment Returns**
    - **Fee Drag**: High fees reduce the compounding effect, significantly impacting long-term wealth accumulation.
    - **Transparent Disclosure**: Ensure full disclosure of all fees before committing to advisory services.

List: Tips for Reducing Advisory Costs

- Opt for fee-only advisors to avoid conflicts of interest.
- Consider hybrid models combining robo-advisors with occasional human advice.
- Regularly review advisor performance against benchmark returns.

Section 3: Risk Management and Emotional Decision-Making

Risk management and controlling emotional responses to market events are vital components of a successful investing strategy.

3.1 Taking on Inappropriate Levels of Risk

Investors often misjudge their risk tolerance, leading to decisions that do not align with their financial goals or comfort levels.

1. **Assessing and Managing Investment Risk**
    - **Risk Assessment Tools**: Use online questionnaires and risk assessment tools to evaluate your comfort level with market fluctuations.
    - **Portfolio Adjustment**: Rebalance periodically to maintain an appropriate risk profile.
2. **Importance of Risk Tolerance Assessment**
    - **Alignment with Goals**: Investments should match your risk tolerance and time horizon.
    - **Avoiding Overexposure**: Avoid high-risk stocks that do not fit your risk profile, particularly in volatile market conditions.
3. **Avoiding Overexposure to High-Risk Investments**
    - **Diversify Risk**: Spread investments across asset classes to reduce specific risk exposure.

- **Safe Havens**: Incorporate safer investments like bonds or dividend-paying stocks to balance high-risk holdings.

Graph 1: Portfolio Risk vs. Reward Balance

A graph plotting risk levels against potential rewards, illustrating the importance of balancing risk tolerance with investment strategy.

Graph 1: Portfolio Risk vs. Reward Balance A graph plotting risk levels against potential rewards, illustrating the importance of balancing risk tolerance with investment strategy.

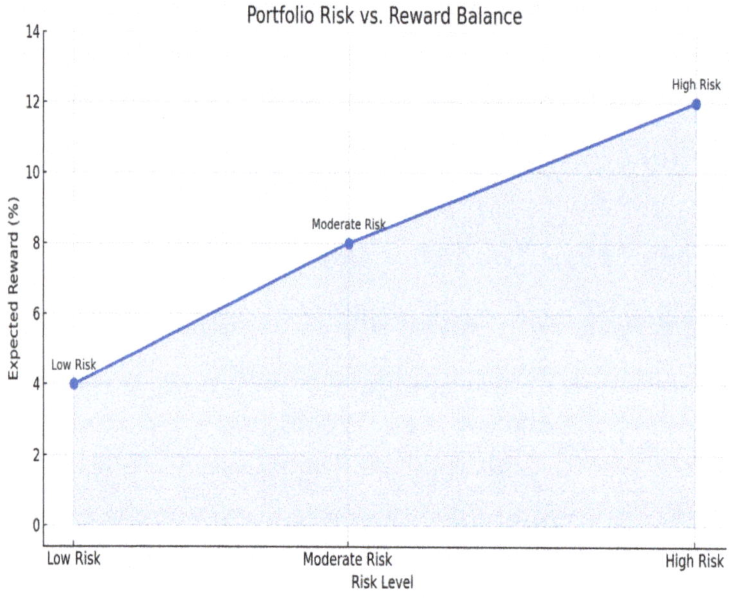

The graph above illustrates the balance between risk and reward in a portfolio. It shows how increasing risk levels, from low to high, are generally associated with higher potential rewards. This visual representation highlights the importance of aligning your risk tolerance with your investment strategy, emphasizing that higher returns usually come with higher risk. The plotted points demonstrate potential expected returns for varying risk levels, making it easier to assess where your comfort zone lies in balancing risk against reward.

3.2 Not Tracking True Investment Performance

Failing to regularly track investment performance can result in missed opportunities for optimization and rebalancing.

1. **Measuring Performance Relative to Financial Plan**
    - **Benchmarking**: Compare your portfolio's performance against relevant benchmarks like the S&P 500.
    - **Performance Metrics**: Use key metrics such as annualized return, Sharpe ratio, and volatility.
2. **Importance of Regular Performance Review**
    - **Periodic Check-ins**: Review your investments quarterly or annually to assess alignment with your financial plan.
    - **Adjustments**: Make necessary changes if certain assets underperform or if your goals shift.
3. **Adjusting Strategy Based on Performance**
    - **Rebalancing**: Shift funds from over-performing sectors to underweighted ones to maintain balance.
    - **Tax-Loss Harvesting**: Use underperforming stocks to offset capital gains and reduce tax liability.

Table 3: Performance Review Checklist

Review Item	Frequency	Key Actions	Tools/Resources
Portfolio Performance	Quarterly	Compare against benchmarks	Financial Planning Software
Risk Assessment	Annually	Re-evaluate risk tolerance	Risk Assessment Tools
Rebalancing	Bi-Annually	Adjust asset allocations	Broker Platform Rebalancing
Tax-Loss Harvesting	Annually	Sell losing positions strategically	Tax Software/Advisor

3.3 Overreacting to Media Coverage and Hype

Media and hype can significantly impact investor behavior, often leading to impulsive decisions that hurt long-term returns.

1. **Distinguishing Valuable Information from Noise**
    - **Information Overload**: The 24/7 news cycle can overwhelm investors with conflicting advice.
    - **Reliable Sources**: Focus on data-driven, reputable sources rather than sensational headlines.
2. **Strategies for Rational Decision-Making**
    - **Investment Thesis**: Stick to your investment plan and avoid knee-jerk reactions to market noise.

- **Pause and Reflect**: Before making decisions, take a moment to assess if the information truly impacts your long-term goals.

3. **Avoiding Emotional Investing**

- **Behavioral Biases**: Be aware of biases such as fear of missing out (FOMO) and loss aversion.
- **Automated Investing**: Consider using automated investing tools to reduce the influence of emotions on your decisions.

Chart 3: Emotional vs. Rational Investment Decisions

A chart comparing the performance of emotion-driven investors versus those who follow a disciplined strategy.

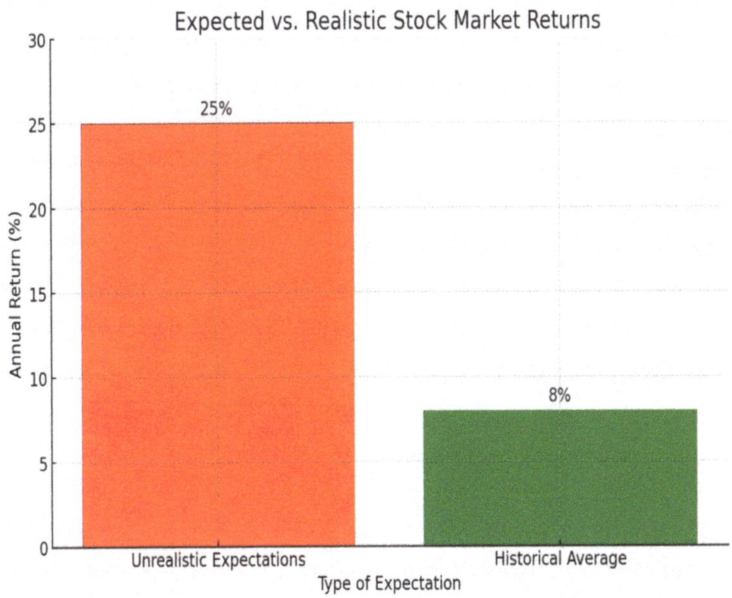

Here is a bar chart illustrating the difference between unrealistic stock market return expectations (e.g., 25%) and realistic historical averages (around 8%). This visual representation highlights the common misconception among investors regarding potential returns, emphasizing the importance of setting reasonable expectations in stock market investing. Let me know if you need further adjustments or additional visualizations!

Avoiding common stock investing mistakes is critical to building long-term wealth. By understanding and mitigating these errors, investors can improve their financial outcomes, manage risks effectively, and stay on course toward their investment goals. The key takeaway is to maintain a disciplined, informed, and objective approach to stock investing, focusing on long-term success rather than short-term gains.

Chapter 8: Maximizing Profits: Make Money with Growth Stocks

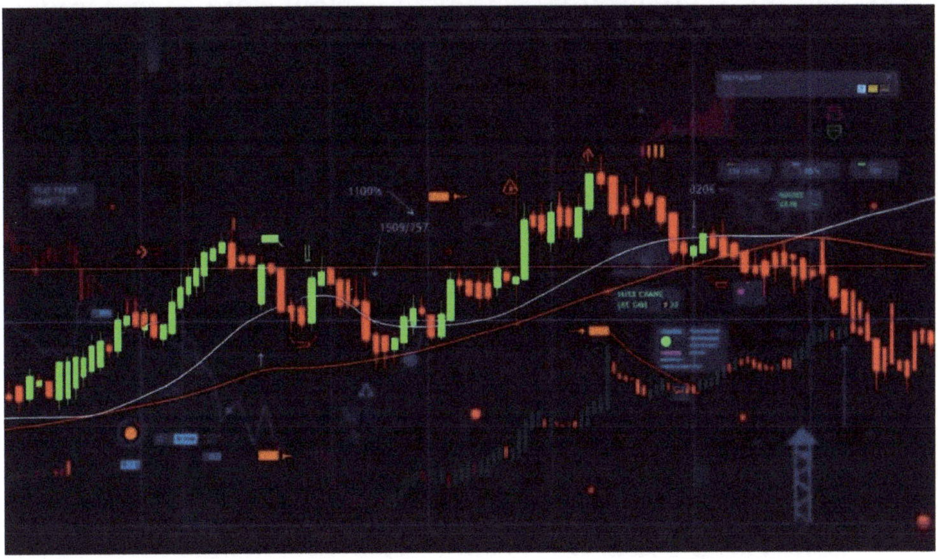

Growth stocks can offer significant returns, but they also come with unique risks. Understanding growth investing and implementing effective strategies can help you capitalize on opportunities while managing potential downsides.

Section 1: Understanding Growth Investing

1.1 Definition of Growth Investing

Growth investing focuses on companies expected to grow significantly faster than the overall market.

- **Key Characteristics of Growth Stocks:** High earnings growth potential, reinvestment of profits into expansion, and innovative products or services.

- **Comparing Growth and Value Investing:** Growth stocks are typically more expensive, with higher price-to-earnings (P/E) ratios, while value stocks are considered undervalued.

Table 3: Growth vs. Value Investing

Feature	Growth Investing	Value Investing
Focus	High growth potential	Undervalued stocks
Risk	Higher due to market volatility	Lower, stable investments
Return Potential	High	Moderate

1.2 Identifying Potential Growth Stocks

- **Analyzing Industry Trends:** Growth stocks often thrive in industries like technology, healthcare, and consumer goods that benefit from innovation and evolving consumer preferences.
- **Assessing Company Financials:** Look for strong revenue growth, positive cash flow, and a solid balance sheet. Avoid companies with unsustainable debt levels.
- **Evaluating Management Quality:** A capable management team is crucial for executing growth strategies and adapting to market changes.

1.3 Factors Driving Growth Stock Performance

- **Innovation and Technological Advancements:** Companies at the forefront of technology often lead growth sectors.

- **Market Demand and Consumer Trends:** Identify companies meeting changing consumer needs and market demand.
- **Regulatory Environment and Government Policies:** Be aware of how regulatory changes might impact growth companies, particularly in industries like biotech and fintech.

Section 2: Risks and Diversification Strategies

2.1 Risks Associated with Growth Investing

Growth stocks are known for their potential to deliver high returns, but they come with risks.

- **Market Volatility and Growth Stocks:** Growth stocks are highly sensitive to market conditions and can experience significant price swings.
- **Company-Specific Risks:** High growth expectations mean any negative news can lead to steep declines.
- **Economic and Sector Risks:** Growth sectors can be more affected by economic downturns and sector-specific issues.

2.2 Diversification Strategies for Growth Investors

Diversification can help mitigate some risks associated with growth investing.

- **Sector Diversification:** Spread investments across multiple growth sectors to reduce the impact of downturns in any one area.

- **Geographical Diversification:** Include international growth stocks to capitalize on global opportunities.
- **Market Cap Diversification:** Balance between large-cap growth stocks and small or mid-cap companies for additional growth potential.

2.3 Growth Investing in Different Market Conditions

Adjust your growth investing strategy based on market conditions.

- **Bull Market Strategies:** In a bull market, growth stocks tend to outperform. Focus on companies with strong earnings momentum.
- **Bear Market Strategies:** In a downturn, defensive growth stocks, such as those in consumer staples or healthcare, can provide some protection.
- **Adjusting Strategies Based on Market Conditions:** Use technical and fundamental analysis to identify buying opportunities during market corrections.

Section 3: Case Studies and Common Mistakes

3.1 Case Studies: Successful Growth Stock Investments

Learn from past successful growth investments to understand what makes a stock a good growth candidate.

- **Analyzing Successful Growth Investments:** Review case studies of companies like Amazon, Apple, and Tesla to understand how innovation, market leadership, and financial discipline contributed to their success.

- **Key Lessons from Case Studies:** Consistent earnings growth, strong management, and market leadership are critical factors in successful growth investing.
- **Applying Insights to Your Investment Strategy:** Use insights from successful companies to identify future growth opportunities.

3.2 Common Mistakes to Avoid in Growth Investing

Avoid these common pitfalls to improve your chances of success.

- **Chasing High-Flying Stocks:** Avoid buying stocks solely because they have risen rapidly in price without fundamental support.
- **Neglecting Fundamentals:** Focus on companies with strong financials and sustainable growth strategies.
- **Overconcentration in a Single Stock or Sector:** Diversify to avoid excessive risk exposure.

3.3 The Role of Research and Due Diligence

Thorough research is crucial to making informed growth investment decisions.

- **Staying Informed about Market Trends:** Regularly follow industry news, analyst reports, and economic indicators.
- **Analyzing Company Reports and Financial Statements:** Use financial analysis to evaluate a company's health and growth potential.

- **Growth Investing Tools and Resources:** Leverage investment tools, such as stock screeners, financial news platforms, and investment research services.

By understanding the common mistakes in stock investing and applying disciplined growth strategies, investors can maximize their returns while managing risk. Consistent research, clear goal setting, and diversification are key elements of a successful investment strategy.

Chapter 9: Make Money with ETFs: Smart Investing Strategies

Section 1: Understanding Exchange-Traded Funds (ETFs)

1.1 What Are ETFs and How Do They Work?

Definition and Structure of ETFs

Exchange-Traded Funds (ETFs) are investment funds that trade on stock exchanges, much like individual stocks. They hold a collection of assets such as stocks, bonds, or commodities and offer investors a way to gain exposure to a broad range of securities within a single investment vehicle.

- **Structure:** ETFs are structured to track the performance of a specific index, sector, or asset class. They are typically managed by a fund provider and are traded throughout the day on stock exchanges.
- **Creation and Redemption:** ETFs are created and redeemed through a process involving authorized participants who exchange blocks of ETF shares for the underlying assets and vice versa.

How ETFs Are Traded

- **Trading Mechanism:** ETFs are bought and sold on stock exchanges at market prices, which may differ from their net asset value (NAV). Investors can place market or limit orders to buy or sell ETF shares.
- **Liquidity:** ETFs offer liquidity as they are traded on major stock exchanges, allowing investors to enter or exit positions throughout the trading day.

Types of ETFs (Equity, Bond, Commodity)

1. **Equity ETFs:** These ETFs invest primarily in stocks. They can be broad-based, tracking major indices like the S&P 500, or sector-specific, focusing on particular industries like technology or healthcare.

2. **Bond ETFs:** These ETFs invest in fixed-income securities such as government or corporate bonds. They offer income through interest payments and can be used to diversify fixed-income investments.
3. **Commodity ETFs:** These ETFs invest in commodities like gold, oil, or agricultural products. They provide a way to gain exposure to commodity markets without directly purchasing the physical assets.

Chart 1: Types of ETFs

Description: This chart illustrates the different types of ETFs and their investment focus.

1.2 Advantages of ETFs for Beginning Investors

Low Costs and Fees

- **Expense Ratios:** ETFs generally have lower expense ratios compared to mutual funds due to their passive management style.
- **Trading Costs:** Investors incur trading commissions, but these are typically lower compared to the management fees of actively managed funds.

Diversification Benefits

- **Broad Exposure:** ETFs provide diversification by holding a wide range of securities within a single fund, reducing individual stock risk.
- **Variety:** Investors can access various asset classes, sectors, or geographic regions through a single ETF.

Flexibility and Liquidity

- **Trading Flexibility:** ETFs can be traded throughout the day, allowing investors to respond to market movements.
- **Liquidity:** ETFs are generally liquid, with bid-ask spreads reflecting market demand and supply.

Table 1: ETF Advantages

Advantage	Description
Low Costs	Lower expense ratios and trading costs
Diversification	Exposure to a broad range of securities
Flexibility	Ability to trade throughout the day

Description: This table summarizes the key advantages of investing in ETFs.

1.3 Choosing the Right ETFs for Your Investment Goals

Stock ETFs vs. Bond ETFs

- **Stock ETFs:** Suitable for investors seeking growth through equity exposure. They track stock indices or specific sectors.
- **Bond ETFs:** Appropriate for income-focused investors looking for fixed-income returns and reduced interest rate risk.

Sector-Specific ETFs

- **Sector ETFs:** Focus on specific industry sectors such as technology, healthcare, or energy. They are useful for targeting particular market segments.

Commodity ETFs

- **Commodity ETFs:** Provide exposure to physical commodities or commodity futures. They are used for diversification and hedging against inflation.

Chart 2: ETF Selection Criteria

Here's a comparison chart outlining the selection criteria for Stock ETFs vs. Bond ETFs:

Criteria	Stock ETFs	Bond ETFs
Objective	Growth, capital appreciation	Income, capital preservation
Risk Level	Higher (market volatility)	Lower (interest rate, credit risk)
Expected Returns	Potentially higher, linked to equity markets	Generally lower, linked to interest rates
Expense Ratio	Moderate to high	Generally lower
Income Generation	Lower, depends on dividends	Higher, depends on bond yields
Diversification	Broad sector/market exposure	Exposure to various bond types (government, corporate)
Time Horizon	Long-term (5+ years)	Short to medium-term
Sensitivity to Interest Rates	Low	High (prices fall when rates rise)
Tax Efficiency	Higher, often lower dividends	Lower, due to bond coupon payments
Liquidity	High	Varies, lower for less liquid

Criteria	Stock ETFs	Bond ETFs
		bonds
Volatility	High, depends on the market	Lower, but sensitive to rate changes
Yield	Varies (lower dividends)	Higher (interest payments)
Use in Portfolios	Growth, wealth accumulation	Stability, income generation
Common Sectors	Technology, Healthcare, Financials	Government, Corporate, High-Yield Bonds

This chart provides a quick overview of the key factors to consider when choosing between Stock ETFs and Bond ETFs, helping investors align their choices with their financial goals and risk tolerance. Let me know if you need further adjustments or additional criteria!

Description: This chart helps investors compare different types of ETFs based on their investment goals.

Section 2: Dollar-Cost Averaging and Asset Allocation

2.1 Dollar-Cost Averaging: A Beginner-Friendly ETF Strategy

How Dollar-Cost Averaging Works

- **Definition:** Dollar-cost averaging involves investing a fixed amount of money at regular intervals, regardless of the ETF's price. This approach reduces the impact of market volatility on the overall investment.
- **Mechanism:** By buying more shares when prices are low and fewer shares when prices are high, investors average out their purchase price over time.

Benefits of Dollar-Cost Averaging for ETF Investors

- **Reduced Timing Risk:** Minimizes the risk of investing a large sum at an inopportune time.
- **Simplicity:** Easy to implement and manage, making it suitable for beginners.

Implementing Dollar-Cost Averaging with ETFs

- **Automatic Investments:** Set up automatic transfers to invest a fixed amount in ETFs on a regular basis.
- **Consistency:** Maintain a consistent investment schedule, regardless of market conditions.

Chart 3: Dollar-Cost Averaging Impact

Here's a chart that outlines the impact of Dollar-Cost Averaging (DCA) compared to Lump-Sum Investing, highlighting key aspects of each strategy:

Criteria	Dollar-Cost Averaging (DCA)	Lump-Sum Investing
Definition	Investing a fixed amount regularly over time	Investing a large sum all at once
Market Timing Risk	Reduces risk by spreading investments across different market conditions	Higher risk due to immediate exposure to market conditions
Volatility Impact	Mitigates impact of short-term volatility	Fully exposed to immediate market swings
Emotional Comfort	Reduces anxiety by avoiding investing all funds at market highs	Can be stressful if markets decline right after investing
Average Purchase Cost	Can lower average cost per share over time by buying dips	One-time cost based on market price at the time of investment
Potential Returns	Generally lower in strong, rising markets	Higher in consistently rising markets

Criteria	Dollar-Cost Averaging (DCA)	Lump-Sum Investing
Discipline Requirement	Encourages consistent investing behavior	Less discipline needed after the initial investment
Cash Drag	Funds waiting to be invested may miss out on potential returns	Fully invested immediately, no cash drag
Ideal Market Condition	Best for volatile or declining markets	Best for long-term bull markets
Flexibility	Easy to adjust amounts and timing	Less flexibility once invested
Emotional Bias Control	Helps control fear and greed by automating investments	Susceptible to emotional decisions based on market swings
Overall Risk	Lower due to gradual market entry	Higher due to immediate market exposure
Use Case	Suitable for risk-averse investors or those starting with limited funds	Suitable for investors with a lump sum and long time horizon

This chart illustrates how Dollar-Cost Averaging can smooth out the impact of market volatility and make investing less stressful, while Lump-Sum Investing can maximize returns in upward-trending markets but carries higher risk.

Description: This chart demonstrates how dollar-cost averaging can smooth out the impact of market fluctuations.

2.2 Asset Allocation with ETFs

Importance of Asset Allocation

- **Diversification:** Spreading investments across various asset classes to reduce risk and improve returns.
- **Risk Management:** Helps manage risk by balancing investments in stocks, bonds, and other assets.

Creating a Balanced ETF Portfolio

- **Asset Mix:** Allocate investments across different ETFs representing various asset classes and sectors.
- **Rebalancing:** Periodically review and adjust the portfolio to maintain the desired asset allocation.

Rebalancing and Adjusting Allocations

- **Rebalancing Frequency:** Regularly rebalance the portfolio to ensure it aligns with your investment goals and risk tolerance.
- **Adjustments:** Make adjustments based on changes in market conditions or personal financial goals.

Table 2: Sample ETF Portfolio Allocation

Asset Class	Percentage	Example ETFs
Equities	60%	S&P 500 ETF, Technology ETF
Bonds	30%	Government Bond ETF, Corporate Bond ETF
Commodities	10%	Gold ETF, Oil ETF

Description: This table shows a sample ETF portfolio allocation across asset classes.

2.3 Swing Trading and Sector Rotation

Attributes of ETFs Suitable for Swing Trading

- **Volatility:** Look for ETFs with higher volatility for potential short-term gains.

- **Liquidity:** Ensure the ETF has sufficient trading volume for ease of entry and exit.

Adapting Your ETF Portfolio to Market Trends

- **Market Trends:** Adjust ETF holdings based on prevailing market trends and economic conditions.
- **Trend Analysis:** Use technical analysis to identify trends and make informed trading decisions.

Sector Rotation Strategies

- **Sector Rotation:** Shift investments among sectors based on economic cycles and market performance.
- **Examples:** Increase exposure to defensive sectors during downturns and growth sectors during expansions.

Chart 4: Sector Rotation Strategy

Here's a chart outlining the key aspects of the Sector Rotation Strategy:

Criteria	Sector Rotation Strategy
Definition	A strategy that involves moving investments among different sectors based on economic and market cycles
Objective	To capitalize on sector performance based on economic trends
Approach	Active management, frequent adjustments based on market conditions

Criteria	Sector Rotation Strategy
Market Timing	Requires accurate market timing to switch sectors effectively
Risk Level	Higher due to the need for frequent adjustments and market predictions
Potential Returns	Can be high if sector selection and timing are accurate
Investment Horizon	Typically medium to long-term, with adjustments as market conditions change
Research Required	High; involves analysis of economic indicators and sector performance
Sector Analysis	Requires understanding of various sectors and their economic sensitivities
Flexibility	High; ability to adjust allocations based on market conditions
Costs	Higher transaction costs due to frequent trading
Skill Level	Requires significant expertise and experience in market analysis
Performance Monitoring	Regular monitoring and analysis of sector performance
Common Tools	Sector ETFs, mutual funds, economic indicators, and market research reports
Economic Indicators	Key indicators include GDP growth, inflation rates, interest rates, and employment data
Risk Management	Diversification and careful sector selection to mitigate risk
Historical Performance	Historically, can outperform broad market indices during specific economic phases

This chart provides a snapshot of the Sector Rotation Strategy, focusing on its objectives, risks, potential returns, and requirements.

Description: This chart outlines a sector rotation strategy based on economic cycles.

Section 3: Hedging, Income, and Tax Implications

3.1 Hedging Your Portfolio with ETFs

Using Broad Market ETFs to Hedge Downside Risk

- **Broad Market ETFs:** Use ETFs that track major indices (e.g., S&P 500) as a hedge against market declines.
- **Inverse ETFs:** Consider inverse or leveraged ETFs for more direct hedging strategies.

Strategies for Hedging with ETFs

- **Hedging Allocation:** Allocate a portion of your portfolio to hedging ETFs to manage potential losses.
- **Regular Review:** Continuously assess the effectiveness of your hedging strategy and make adjustments as needed.

Evaluating Hedge Effectiveness

- **Performance Tracking:** Monitor the performance of your hedging ETFs relative to market conditions.
- **Adjustments:** Make necessary adjustments based on changes in market volatility or your investment goals.

Chart 5: Hedging with ETFs

Here's a chart outlining how to hedge with ETFs, including different strategies and considerations:

Criteria	Hedging with ETFs
Definition	Using ETFs to manage or mitigate risk in an investment portfolio
Objective	To protect against potential losses in the underlying investments

Criteria	Hedging with ETFs
Common ETF Types for Hedging	Inverse ETFs, leveraged ETFs, sector-specific ETFs, commodity ETFs, bond ETFs
Inverse ETFs	Designed to move in the opposite direction of the underlying index, used to hedge against declines
Leveraged ETFs	Aim to amplify the returns of an underlying index, can be used to hedge by betting against an index
Sector-Specific ETFs	Target specific sectors that may outperform in a downturn or market decline
Commodity ETFs	Invest in commodities like gold or oil, which may act as a safe haven during market volatility
Bond ETFs	Invest in government or high-quality corporate bonds to provide stability and income
Costs	Management fees, potential bid-ask spreads, and transaction costs
Risk Level	Varies; inverse and leveraged ETFs can be highly volatile, while bond ETFs and commodity ETFs may offer lower risk
Usage	Short-term hedging to protect against market declines or long-term protection in uncertain times
Liquidity	Important to choose ETFs with high liquidity to avoid large bid-ask spreads
Time Horizon	Short-term for tactical hedging or longer-term for strategic protection
Implementation	Direct purchase of hedging ETFs or incorporating into a broader asset allocation strategy
Monitoring	Regularly review the performance of hedging positions and adjust as needed
Potential Drawbacks	Over-hedging can reduce potential gains, and some ETFs may not perfectly track their intended hedge
Example Strategy	Use inverse ETFs to hedge against potential

Criteria	Hedging with ETFs
	equity market declines, or commodity ETFs for inflation protection

This chart highlights how different types of ETFs can be used for hedging purposes, along with their associated risks, costs, and implementation considerations.

Description: This chart illustrates different hedging strategies using ETFs.

3.2 Generating Income with ETFs

Dividend-Paying Equity ETFs

- **Definition:** ETFs that invest in dividend-paying stocks, providing regular income through dividends.
- **Examples:** High dividend yield ETFs or dividend aristocrats ETFs.

Bond Fund ETFs

- **Definition:** ETFs that invest in bonds, offering fixed-income returns through interest payments.
- **Types:** Government, municipal, and corporate bond ETFs.

Real Estate Investment Trust (REIT) ETFs

- **Definition:** ETFs that invest in REITs, which own or finance income-producing real estate. They provide income through rental yields and capital appreciation.

- **Examples:** Residential, commercial, and diversified REIT ETFs.

Table 3: Income-Generating ETFs

ETF Type	Income Source	Example ETFs
Dividend ETFs	Stock dividends	Dividend Aristocrats ETF, High Yield Dividend ETF
Bond ETFs	Interest payments	Government Bond ETF, Corporate Bond ETF
REIT ETFs	Real estate income	Residential REIT ETF, Commercial REIT ETF

Description: This table shows different types of income-generating ETFs and examples.

3.3 Tax Implications of ETF Investing

Capital Gains Tax on ETF Profits

- **Realization of Gains:** Capital gains tax is applied on profits made from selling ETF shares at a higher price than the purchase price.
- **Tax Rates:** The rate depends on the holding period and your income tax bracket.

Taxation of Interest and Dividend Income

- **Interest Income:** Taxed as ordinary income when received from bond ETFs.
- **Dividend Income:** Qualified dividends are taxed at a lower rate compared to ordinary income.

Comparing Fees and Expenses of Different ETFs

- **Expense Ratios:** Compare expense ratios to ensure cost-effectiveness.
- **Other Fees:** Consider trading commissions and bid-ask spreads in your cost analysis.

Chart 6: ETF Tax Considerations

Here's a chart outlining the key tax considerations for ETFs:

Criteria	ETF Tax Considerations
Capital Gains	ETFs generally have lower capital gains distributions compared to mutual funds due to their structure
Dividend Taxes	Dividends from ETFs are taxed as ordinary income or qualified dividends depending on the type and holding period
Qualified Dividends	Dividends that meet IRS requirements are taxed at the lower long-term capital gains rate
Ordinary Income	Non-qualified dividends are taxed at ordinary income rates, which can be higher than capital gains rates
Tax Efficiency	ETFs are often tax-efficient due to the "in-kind" creation and redemption process, which helps avoid triggering capital gains
Tax Loss Harvesting	ETFs can be used to offset gains with losses through tax loss harvesting strategies
Fund Type Impact	Different ETF types (e.g., equity, bond, commodity) have different tax implications based on their income and gains
Interest Income	Bond ETFs may distribute interest income, which is taxed as ordinary income
Foreign Income	Income from international ETFs may be subject to foreign taxes, which can sometimes be claimed as a credit on U.S. tax returns

Criteria	ETF Tax Considerations
Tax Reporting	ETFs provide tax documents such as 1099 forms to report dividends, capital gains, and interest income
Wash Sale Rule	Applies to ETF investments as well; selling an ETF at a loss and repurchasing within 30 days may disallow the loss for tax purposes
Tax-Advantaged Accounts	ETFs held in tax-advantaged accounts (e.g., IRAs, 401(k)s) are not subject to annual taxes on gains and dividends
State Taxes	State tax treatment may vary; some states may tax capital gains and dividends differently
Fund Complexity	More complex ETFs (e.g., those involving derivatives) may have unique tax considerations and require careful review

This chart highlights the primary tax considerations for ETF investors, including the impact of different types of income and strategies for tax efficiency.

Description: This chart outlines key tax considerations for ETF investors.

Chapter 10 How Does a Company Benefit by Having Their Stock Listed on An Exchange

When a company lists its stock on an exchange, it gains several strategic, financial, and operational advantages that can significantly enhance its market position and long-term growth prospects. Here's an expanded view of how a company benefits from having its stock listed on an exchange:

1. Access to Capital for Growth and Expansion

- **Raising Funds:** The primary benefit of listing is the ability to raise significant amounts of capital by issuing new shares to the public. This is often a more efficient and cost-effective way to fund growth compared to other financing options like bank loans or private equity, which may come with higher interest rates or more restrictive terms.

- **Debt Reduction:** The funds raised can also be used to pay down existing debt, reducing financial leverage and improving the company’s balance sheet. Lower debt levels can lead to better credit ratings, which further reduces borrowing costs.

2. Enhanced Visibility and Credibility

- **Brand Recognition:** Listing on a major stock exchange, like the NYSE or NASDAQ, elevates the company's profile. This increased visibility can boost brand recognition and customer trust, which can translate into higher sales and market share.
- **Investor Confidence:** Being listed signals to investors that the company meets stringent regulatory and financial reporting standards, enhancing its credibility. This can attract institutional investors who often avoid private or unlisted companies due to transparency issues.

3. Liquidity for Shareholders

- **Ease of Buying and Selling:** Stock exchanges provide a centralized and regulated market where shares can be easily traded. This liquidity is attractive to investors because it allows them to enter and exit their investments efficiently, often at fair market prices.
- **Valuation Transparency:** Regular trading of shares establishes a market-driven valuation of the company, which can be more accurate and transparent than private

valuations. This continuous pricing helps both the company and its investors make informed financial decisions.

4. Employee Incentives and Retention

- **Stock Options and Equity Compensation:** Public companies can offer stock options, restricted stock units (RSUs), or other equity-based incentives to employees, aligning their interests with shareholders. This can be a powerful tool for motivating employees and retaining top talent, as they directly benefit from the company's success.
- **Employee Morale and Ownership:** Employee stock ownership programs (ESOPs) can improve morale and foster a culture of ownership within the company, leading to increased productivity and commitment.

5. Acquisition Currency and Strategic Flexibility

- **Using Stock for Acquisitions:** Listed shares can be used as a form of currency in mergers and acquisitions, allowing the company to acquire other businesses without using cash. This flexibility can accelerate growth and help the company enter new markets or acquire complementary technologies.
- **Strategic Partnerships:** A publicly traded status can make the company a more attractive partner for strategic alliances and joint ventures, as partners may view listed companies as more stable and financially transparent.

6. Improved Corporate Governance and Operational Discipline

- **Regulatory Compliance:** Public companies are subject to rigorous reporting and governance standards, including regular financial disclosures, audits, and adherence to strict corporate governance codes. These requirements can improve operational discipline, reduce management inefficiencies, and enhance investor confidence.
- **Accountability:** Being accountable to a broader group of stakeholders, including institutional investors and regulators, can drive management to make decisions that are in the best long-term interest of the company and its shareholders.

7. Market Perception and Competitive Advantage

- **Enhanced Market Standing:** Being publicly listed can enhance a company's reputation, making it appear larger and more established compared to privately held competitors. This perception can be particularly beneficial when competing for contracts, partnerships, or entering new markets.
- **Benchmarking Performance:** The transparency of being a publicly listed company allows for benchmarking against industry peers, providing valuable insights into how the company performs relative to competitors. This can help management identify areas for improvement and implement strategic adjustments.

8. Diversification of Ownership

- **Reduced Concentration Risk:** By broadening its ownership base through public trading, a company can reduce the concentration of ownership risk among founders or a small group of private investors. This diversified ownership can stabilize the shareholder base and reduce the impact of any single investor's decisions on the company's stock price.
- **Wider Shareholder Engagement:** Public companies have the opportunity to engage with a broad range of stakeholders, including retail investors, institutional investors, and analysts, which can provide valuable feedback and insights into market expectations.

9. Potential for Future Fundraising

- **Follow-on Offerings:** Once listed, companies have easier access to capital markets for future fundraising through secondary offerings. This ongoing access to capital can support continued growth, innovation, and expansion.
- **Debt Financing Benefits:** Publicly traded companies often find it easier to secure loans and lines of credit at more favorable terms because lenders view them as more transparent and creditworthy.

10. Exit Strategy for Early Investors

- **Liquidity for Founders and Early Investors:** Listing provides an exit strategy for founders, venture capitalists, and early investors, allowing them to realize returns on their investments. This liquidity event can be an essential part of the investment lifecycle for private equity and venture capital funds.

Overall, having stock listed on an exchange offers companies numerous advantages that extend beyond immediate financial gains. It strengthens the company's ability to grow, attract investors, and compete in the global marketplace, making it a pivotal step for many businesses aiming to scale and succeed.

Chapter 11 How to pick stocks like Warren Buffett

To invest like Warren Buffett, it's crucial to delve deeper into his investment philosophy and strategy. Buffett's approach is rooted in value investing, a concept popularized by his mentor, Benjamin Graham, and further refined over decades of successful investing. Here's a comprehensive guide on how to pick stocks like Warren Buffett, with more detailed insights into his key principles:

1. Invest in What You Understand

- **Focus on Your Circle of Competence:** Buffett advises investors to stay within their "circle of competence" — the industries and businesses they understand well. This means concentrating on sectors where you have knowledge or can easily grasp the business model. Avoid investments that seem complex or outside your expertise, as these can lead to costly mistakes.

- **Example:** Buffett often invests in consumer goods companies like Coca-Cola because he understands their business model, market, and growth potential.

2. Look for Companies with Strong Moats

- **Understand Competitive Advantages:** A strong moat can be a brand name, proprietary technology, exclusive distribution channels, or superior cost structures that keep competitors at bay. Buffett seeks companies that have a durable competitive edge, making it difficult for rivals to take market share.
- **Example:** Buffett's investment in Apple is based on its brand loyalty, ecosystem, and high customer retention, which create a strong moat.

3. Evaluate the Management Team

- **Integrity and Competence:** Buffett emphasizes the importance of investing in companies run by ethical and capable managers who are aligned with shareholder interests. He values leaders who are transparent, have a clear vision, and are committed to the company's long-term success.
- **Owner's Mentality:** Look for management that behaves like owners of the company, focusing on sustainable growth rather than short-term stock performance.
- **Example:** Buffett's long-term investment in Berkshire Hathaway's subsidiaries often hinges on his faith in the leaders running those businesses.

4. Focus on Financial Health

- **Analyze Key Metrics:** Buffett pays close attention to financial metrics such as Return on Equity (ROE), Debt-to-Equity ratio, and profit margins. He prefers companies with high ROE, low debt, and consistent earnings growth, as these indicate efficient and financially sound operations.

- **Steady Earnings:** Companies with consistent earnings over time are more predictable and less risky. Buffett avoids companies with volatile earnings, as this indicates instability.
- **Example:** Buffett's investment in American Express was driven by its strong financial performance and reliable revenue streams.

5. Buy at a Discount to Intrinsic Value

- **Margin of Safety:** One of Buffett's cornerstone principles is buying stocks when they are undervalued compared to their intrinsic worth. This approach provides a buffer against errors in judgment and market downturns.
- **Intrinsic Value Calculation:** Use valuation methods such as discounted cash flow (DCF) analysis, which involves forecasting future cash flows and discounting them to their present value. Compare this intrinsic value to the current market price to identify undervalued stocks.
- **Example:** Buffett's purchase of Coca-Cola shares in the 1980s was based on his belief that the company was significantly undervalued relative to its future cash flow potential.

6. Long-Term Perspective

- **Buy-and-Hold Strategy:** Buffett famously said, "Our favorite holding period is forever." This means investing in companies that you believe will perform well over the long term and resisting the urge to sell based on short-term market fluctuations.
- **Avoid Market Timing:** Buffett does not attempt to time the market but instead focuses on the business's intrinsic value, believing that strong companies will deliver returns over time regardless of short-term market movements.
- **Example:** His investment in The Coca-Cola Company has been held for decades, showcasing his commitment to a long-term approach.

7. Look for Consistent Earnings

- **Predictability of Earnings:** Companies with a track record of stable and growing earnings are often more reliable investments. Buffett avoids businesses with unpredictable or fluctuating earnings because they carry higher risk and uncertainty.
- **Historical Performance Matters:** Look at the company's past performance to gauge its resilience in different economic environments.
- **Example:** Buffett's investments in utility companies like MidAmerican Energy are based on their stable and predictable earnings streams.

8. Avoid High Debt

- **Financial Flexibility:** Companies with low debt levels are generally in a better position to handle economic downturns and reinvest in growth. High debt can burden a company, making it vulnerable to interest rate hikes and economic stress.
- **Debt-to-Equity Ratio:** Analyze the Debt-to-Equity ratio to assess the company's leverage. Buffett prefers companies with manageable debt levels, allowing them to navigate tough times without compromising on growth.
- **Example:** Buffett's investment in Kraft Heinz faced challenges due to the company's high leverage, underscoring the importance of manageable debt.

9. Check for Strong Cash Flow

- **Importance of Free Cash Flow:** A strong cash flow allows a company to invest in new opportunities, pay dividends, buy back shares, and reduce debt. It is a key indicator of financial health and operational efficiency.

- **Reinvestment Potential:** Companies with solid cash flow can reinvest in their business, fund new projects, and enhance shareholder value, making them attractive to Buffett.
- **Example:** Apple's robust free cash flow has been a significant factor in Buffett's large stake in the company, providing a steady stream of returns.

10. Stay Patient and Disciplined

- **Emotional Control:** Buffett's success is largely due to his disciplined approach and ability to remain calm during market volatility. He avoids impulsive decisions and sticks to his strategy, even when the market moves against him.
- **Focus on Fundamentals:** Buffett advises focusing on the fundamentals of a business rather than market noise, headlines, or short-term price movements.
- **Example:** During the financial crisis of 2008, Buffett's calm demeanor and steadfast adherence to his principles allowed him to make strategic investments when others were panicking.

Additional Tips to Invest Like Buffett:

- **Read Annual Reports:** Buffett is known for his deep dive into annual reports and financial statements, which helps him understand the intricacies of a company's operations and financial health.
- **Learn Continuously:** Buffett spends hours each day reading and staying informed about various industries and market conditions. He believes that continuous learning is crucial for successful investing.
- **Diversify, But Not Too Much:** Buffett diversifies his portfolio but not excessively. He prefers a concentrated portfolio of high-quality businesses rather than spreading investments too thinly across many companies.

By adhering to these principles and adopting a thoughtful, long-term approach, you can start investing like Warren Buffett, focusing on quality businesses, disciplined buying, and holding for the long run.

Chapter 12: The Best Place to Open Up a Brokerage Account

Choosing the best place to open a brokerage account depends on your investment goals, trading experience, and the types of services you need. Here are some of the best brokerage firms to consider, each with its own strengths:

1. Charles Schwab

- **Best For:** Beginners and all-around investors.
- **Key Features:** No account minimums, $0 commission on stock and ETF trades, extensive research tools, a wide range of investment options, and excellent customer service.
- **Pros:**
    - User-friendly platforms for both beginners and advanced traders.
    - Access to a vast library of educational resources.
    - Robust research and analytic tools.
    - Fractional shares available for investing in high-priced stocks.
- **Cons:** Some mutual funds may have higher expense ratios compared to others.

2. Fidelity Investments

- **Best For:** Long-term investors, beginners, and retirement savers.

- **Key Features:** $0 commissions on stocks, ETFs, and options; no account minimums; excellent customer service; and extensive retirement planning tools.
- **Pros:**
    - Great for retirement accounts (IRAs, 401(k) rollovers).
    - Fractional share investing allows you to buy parts of expensive stocks.
    - A wide array of investment options, including mutual funds with no fees.
- **Cons:** The Active Trader Pro platform, while powerful, may be complex for new investors.

3. E*TRADE

- **Best For:** Active traders and options traders.
- **Key Features:** $0 commission trades, a wide range of investment options, a powerful trading platform (Power E*TRADE), and excellent research tools.
- **Pros:**
    - User-friendly interface with advanced trading features.
    - Great for options trading with competitive pricing.
    - Access to extensive educational resources.
- **Cons:** Some mutual funds may carry transaction fees.

4. TD Ameritrade

- **Best For:** All types of investors, especially active traders.
- **Key Features:** $0 commissions on stock, ETF, and options trades; advanced trading tools through thinkorswim; robust educational resources.
- **Pros:**
    - thinkorswim platform is one of the best for advanced trading and technical analysis.
    - Extensive research and market analysis tools.
    - No account minimums.

- **Cons:** Slightly overwhelming for beginners due to its advanced features.

5. Robinhood

- **Best For:** Mobile-focused traders and beginners who want to trade stocks, ETFs, and cryptocurrencies with zero commissions.
- **Key Features:** Easy-to-use mobile app, no commission fees on stocks, ETFs, options, and crypto trading.
- **Pros:**
    - Simple and intuitive interface.
    - No minimum deposit required.
    - Fractional shares are available, allowing you to start investing with just a few dollars.
- **Cons:** Limited research tools and customer service compared to other brokerages.

6. Webull

- **Best For:** Active traders who want a sleek mobile platform with extended trading hours.
- **Key Features:** $0 commissions, extended hours trading, paper trading, and advanced charting tools.
- **Pros:**
    - User-friendly with comprehensive technical analysis tools.
    - Supports stock, ETF, options, and crypto trading.
    - No account minimums and easy-to-use mobile app.
- **Cons:** Limited access to mutual funds and lack of deep research compared to more established brokerages.

7. Interactive Brokers (IBKR)

- **Best For:** Professional and international traders.
- **Key Features:** Access to a wide range of global markets, low-cost trading fees, and advanced trading tools.
- **Pros:**

    - Competitive pricing with tiered and fixed-rate commissions.
    - Access to a vast selection of global securities and market data.
    - Best-in-class trading platform with advanced analytics.
- **Cons:** The platform can be complex and intimidating for beginners.

8. Vanguard

- **Best For:** Long-term investors and retirement planning.
- **Key Features:** Focuses on low-cost index funds, ETFs, and mutual funds with a strong emphasis on retirement accounts.
- **Pros:**
    - Low expense ratios on funds.
    - Great for IRA accounts and long-term investing.
    - Access to Vanguard's extensive lineup of funds.
- **Cons:** The trading platform is relatively basic compared to other brokers.

Factors to Consider When Choosing a Brokerage Account:

1. **Fees and Commissions:** Look for low or zero commission fees, especially if you plan to trade frequently.
2. **Account Minimums:** Some brokers require a minimum deposit to open an account, while others do not.
3. **Investment Options:** Ensure the broker offers the types of investments you're interested in, such as stocks, ETFs, options, mutual funds, or cryptocurrencies.
4. **Trading Platforms:** Consider the user interface and tools available. Beginners might prefer simpler platforms, while advanced traders may need more powerful tools.
5. **Customer Service:** Access to reliable customer support, either via phone, chat, or email, is crucial.

6. **Research and Education:** Some brokers provide extensive educational resources, market research, and analysis tools to help inform your investment decisions.

Choosing the right brokerage depends on your specific needs, investment style, and the level of service you desire. Comparing these brokers based on your criteria will help you find the best fit for your investing journey.

Here's a chart comparing the top brokerage firms based on key factors to help you choose the best one for your needs:

Brokerage	Best For	Key Features	Pros	Cons
Charles Schwab	Beginners, All-around Investors	$0 commissions, no account minimums, wide investment options	User-friendly, extensive research tools, excellent customer service	Some mutual funds have higher expense ratios
Fidelity Investments	Long-term Investors, Retirement Savers	$0 commissions, no account minimums, great retirement tools	Excellent for retirement, fractional shares, robust research	Active Trader Pro platform can be complex
E*TRADE	Active and Options Traders	$0 commissions, advanced trading platform (Power E*TRADE)	Great options trading, extensive education resources	Some mutual funds have transaction fees
TD Ameritrade	All Types, Especially Active Traders	$0 commissions, thinkorswim	Advanced trading tools, excellent	Overwhelming for beginners

Brokerage	Best For	Key Features	Pros	Cons
		platform, extensive education resources	research and market analysis	
Robinhood	Mobile-Focused Traders, Beginners	Easy-to-use mobile app, $0 commissions on stocks, options, crypto	Simple interface, no minimum deposit, fractional shares available	Limited research tools and customer service
Webull	Active Traders	$0 commissions, advanced charting tools, extended hours trading	Great for technical analysis, paper trading, no account minimums	Limited access to mutual funds, basic research
Interactive Brokers	Professional, International Traders	Low-cost trading, global market access, advanced trading platform	Competitive pricing, access to global markets, advanced analytics	Complex platform, not beginner-friendly
Vanguard	Long-term Investors, Retirement	Low-cost index funds, strong emphasis on retirement accounts	Low expense ratios, great for IRAs, access to Vanguard funds	Basic trading platform

This chart highlights the primary strengths and weaknesses of each brokerage firm, making it easier to decide based on your trading style and investment goals.

Chapter 13: How to Buy Your First Stock

Step 1: Set Up a Brokerage Account

Opening a brokerage account is the essential first step to buying your first stock. This account acts as your gateway to the stock market, allowing you to buy, sell, and hold investments like stocks, ETFs, and mutual funds. Here's how to set up your brokerage account in detail:

Choosing the Right Brokerage Firm

There are numerous brokerage firms available, each offering different features, fee structures, and levels of service. When choosing a broker, consider the following factors:

- **Fees and Commissions:** Many brokers now offer commission-free trading on stocks and ETFs, making investing more affordable. However, it's still important to check for any hidden fees, such as account maintenance fees, transfer fees, or costs associated with trading certain types of assets.
- **Account Minimums:** Some brokers require a minimum deposit to open an account, while others do not. For beginners, it's often best to choose a broker with low or no account minimums so you can start investing with a modest amount of money.
- **User Experience:** Evaluate the broker's website and mobile app to ensure they are user-friendly and easy to navigate. The platform should provide a smooth experience, especially if you are new to investing.

- **Research Tools and Education:** A good brokerage will offer a range of educational resources, including articles, videos, webinars, and stock research tools. These resources can help you learn about investing and make more informed decisions.
- **Customer Service:** Reliable customer service is crucial, especially when you're starting out. Look for brokers that offer multiple contact options like chat, phone, and email support.

Popular brokerage firms to consider include Charles Schwab, Fidelity, TD Ameritrade, Robinhood, and E*TRADE, each catering to different types of investors, from beginners to advanced traders.

Opening Your Account

Once you've chosen your brokerage, visit their website or download their app. The account setup process typically involves the following steps:

1. **Complete the Application:** You'll need to provide personal information such as your name, address, Social Security number, employment details, and financial status. This information helps the broker comply with regulations and determine the suitability of investments for you.
2. **Choose Your Account Type:** Most beginners start with a standard brokerage account, but there are other options like retirement accounts (IRAs), custodial accounts, and margin accounts. A standard account offers the flexibility

to buy and sell investments freely, while retirement accounts have tax advantages but come with specific rules on withdrawals.

3. **Link Your Bank Account:** You'll need to connect a bank account to your brokerage to transfer funds. This process usually involves providing your bank routing and account numbers and may include a verification step where small deposits are made to your bank account for confirmation.
4. **Fund Your Account:** Deposit money into your brokerage account. Many brokers allow instant deposits up to a certain limit, so you can start investing right away. Some brokers also support recurring deposits, allowing you to automate your investment process over time.

Understanding Account Security

Ensure your brokerage uses strong security measures to protect your account. Look for brokers that offer two-factor authentication, biometric logins, and encryption to safeguard your personal information and investments.

Once your brokerage account is set up and funded, you're ready to start researching and buying your first stock.

Step 2: Research Stocks

Researching stocks is crucial before making your first purchase. This step helps you understand what you're investing in, reducing the risk of making uninformed decisions.

Thorough research allows you to identify companies with solid fundamentals, growth potential, and a business model that aligns with your investment goals.

Understanding What You're Buying

When buying a stock, you're purchasing a small ownership stake in a company. Your investment's success depends on the company's performance, so it's vital to understand how it makes money, its competitive position, and its growth prospects. Here's what to look for:

- **Business Model:** Focus on companies whose business models you understand. For instance, if you use a company's products or services frequently (like Apple or Coca-Cola), you're likely more familiar with how they operate.
- **Industry Position:** Assess where the company stands within its industry. Is it a leader with a strong market share, or is it a smaller player trying to gain traction? Industry leaders tend to have more stability and resources to weather economic downturns.
- **Revenue Streams:** Analyze how the company generates income. Does it rely on a single product or service, or does it have multiple streams of revenue? Diversified revenue sources can help a company remain profitable even if one segment faces challenges.

Using Research Tools

Most brokers offer a suite of research tools to help you evaluate stocks. Here are some common tools and how to use them effectively:

- **Stock Screeners:** These tools allow you to filter stocks based on criteria such as market capitalization, sector, P/E ratio, and dividend yield. Use stock screeners to narrow down your options to companies that fit your investing strategy.
- **Financial Statements:** Review the company's financial health by examining its income statement, balance sheet, and cash flow statement. Key metrics to analyze include revenue growth, profit margins, debt levels, and cash flow generation.
- **Analyst Ratings and Reports:** Many brokers provide access to professional analyst reports that include buy, sell, or hold recommendations. While it's wise to consider these insights, always conduct your own research to validate an analyst's opinion.
- **Company News and Press Releases:** Stay updated with the latest news and press releases from the company. Announcements related to earnings, product launches, management changes, or industry developments can significantly impact stock prices.

Key Metrics to Evaluate

- **Price-to-Earnings (P/E) Ratio:** This ratio measures the price of a stock relative to its earnings per share (EPS). A lower P/E may indicate a stock is undervalued, while a higher P/E could suggest it's overvalued or has high growth expectations.

- **Dividend Yield:** If you're looking for income, consider stocks that pay dividends. The dividend yield tells you how much a company pays in dividends relative to its share price.
- **Earnings Growth:** Look for companies with consistent earnings growth, which can signal a healthy and expanding business.
- **Debt Levels:** Companies with high debt levels may struggle during economic downturns, while those with low or manageable debt are generally more stable.

Taking the time to research stocks thoroughly before investing helps ensure you're making informed decisions and sets the foundation for long-term investing success.

Step 3: Decide How Much to Invest

Once you've selected a stock, the next step is to decide how much money you want to invest. Proper allocation is key to managing risk, especially when you're starting out. This step helps you determine an amount that fits your budget and aligns with your risk tolerance and investment goals.

Start Small and Scale Up

For your first stock purchase, it's best to start small. Investing a modest amount allows you to learn the ropes without exposing yourself to significant financial risk. You can always invest more as you become more comfortable and knowledgeable.

- **Assess Your Budget:** Review your personal finances to determine how much you can afford to invest without impacting your daily expenses or emergency savings. A common guideline is to invest money that you won't need for at least the next 3-5 years.
- **Dollar-Cost Averaging:** Consider using dollar-cost averaging, where you invest a fixed amount of money regularly, such as monthly or quarterly. This strategy helps reduce the impact of market volatility by spreading your purchases over time, buying more shares when prices are low and fewer when prices are high.

Diversification

Diversification is a key principle in investing. It involves spreading your investments across different asset classes, sectors, or stocks to minimize risk. Instead of putting all your money into one stock, consider building a diversified portfolio to protect against individual stock volatility.

- **Start with ETFs or Mutual Funds:** If you're unsure about picking individual stocks, consider starting with an ETF (Exchange-Traded Fund) or a mutual fund. These investment vehicles pool money from many investors to buy a diversified mix of stocks, bonds, or other assets, offering instant diversification.
- **Invest in Fractional Shares:** Many brokers now allow you to buy fractional shares, which means you can

purchase a portion of a stock rather than a whole share. This is particularly useful for high-priced stocks like Amazon or Tesla, enabling you to start investing with as little as $10.

Risk Tolerance

Understanding your risk tolerance is critical when deciding how much to invest. Risk tolerance refers to how much loss you can comfortably withstand in pursuit of higher returns. Here's how to assess your risk level:

- **Time Horizon:** The length of time you plan to hold your investment can affect your risk tolerance. If you're investing for retirement decades away, you might be willing to take on more risk than someone investing for a short-term goal.
- **Emotional Comfort:** Consider how you react to market downturns. If a 10% drop in your portfolio would cause you to panic and sell, you might want to invest more conservatively or start with smaller amounts until you build confidence.
- **Investment Goals:** Define what you're investing for, such as retirement, buying a home, or saving for a child's education. Your goals will help determine the appropriate level of risk and the amount you should invest.

By carefully considering how much to invest, you can take a measured approach that aligns with your financial situation and risk appetite, setting you up for a successful start in investing.

Step 4: Choose Your Order Type

After deciding how much to invest, the next step is to choose the type of order you'll use to buy your stock. The type of order determines how your trade is executed and at what price. Here's a detailed explanation of the most common order types:

Market Order

- **Definition:** A market order is an order to buy or sell a stock immediately at the best available current price. Market orders are typically executed quickly, making them ideal for stocks with high liquidity.
- **When to Use:** Use market orders when you want to ensure the trade is executed promptly and you're comfortable with the current price. This order type is straightforward and often preferred by beginners.
- **Pros and Cons:**
    - **Pros:** Fast execution, simplicity, suitable for liquid stocks.
    - **Cons:** Price uncertainty, as the trade will execute at the next available price, which might be slightly different from what you see, especially in fast-moving markets.

Limit Order

- **Definition:** A limit order sets a specific price at which you're willing to buy or sell a stock. The trade will only execute if the stock reaches your specified price, giving you more control over the price at which you buy or sell.

- **When to Use:** Use limit orders when you want to buy a stock at a specific price and are willing to wait for the market to reach that price. Limit orders are particularly useful in volatile markets or when trading less liquid stocks.
- **Pros and Cons:**
    - **Pros:** Price control, avoids overpaying or underselling.
    - **Cons:** No guarantee of execution, especially if the stock doesn't reach your set price.

Stop Order (Stop-Loss and Stop-Limit)

- **Definition:** A stop order becomes a market order once the stock reaches a predetermined price, called the stop price. This type of order can be used to limit losses or protect gains.
- **Stop-Loss Order:** Triggers a market order when the stock hits the stop price, selling the stock to prevent further losses.
- **Stop-Limit Order:** Becomes a limit order once the stop price is reached, executing only at the limit price or better.
- **When to Use:** Use stop orders if you want to limit potential losses or set an automatic point at which to exit a position.
- **Pros and Cons:**
    - **Pros:** Helps manage risk, automates selling decisions.

- **Cons:** No guarantee of execution with stop-limit orders, particularly in fast-moving markets.

Other Order Types

- **Trailing Stop Order:** Sets a dynamic stop price that moves with the stock's price, helping lock in gains while limiting losses.
- **Good-'Til-Canceled (GTC):** Allows the order to remain active until it's filled or canceled, unlike day orders that expire at the end of the trading day.

Understanding these order types helps you control how your trades are executed, giving you more control over your investments and protecting your portfolio from unwanted price movements.

Step 5: Buy the Stock

Now that you've set up your account, researched your stock, decided how much to invest, and selected your order type, it's time to execute your first trade. Buying your first stock is an exciting milestone, and it's straightforward once you know the steps.

Placing Your Trade

1. **Log into Your Brokerage Account:** Access your brokerage account via the website or mobile app.
2. **Search for the Stock:** Use the search bar to find the stock you want to buy by entering its ticker symbol (e.g., AAPL for Apple) or the company name. You'll be taken

to the stock's detailed page, showing its current price, performance charts, and key statistics.

3. **Click 'Buy':** Find the 'Buy' button on the stock's page. This will open an order form where you'll specify your trade details.
4. **Enter the Number of Shares or Dollar Amount:** If buying whole shares, enter the number of shares you wish to purchase. If your broker supports fractional shares, you can enter the dollar amount you want to invest instead.
5. **Select Your Order Type:** Choose between a market order, limit order, or other order types based on your strategy and comfort level with the stock's price.
6. **Review Your Order:** Carefully check all the details, including the total cost, fees (if any), and the type of order you're placing. Confirming your order ensures you understand the trade before executing it.
7. **Submit Your Order:** Click 'Submit' or 'Place Order' to execute your trade. Your broker will process the order based on the criteria you specified. If using a market order, the trade will usually be filled immediately.

Order Confirmation and Trade Execution

After submitting your order, you'll receive a confirmation notice indicating that the trade has been executed. This confirmation will include the final price per share, the number of shares purchased, and any applicable fees. The stock will then appear in your portfolio, showing your ownership stake.

What Happens Next?

Once your trade is executed, you officially own your first stock! You can track your stock's performance in your brokerage account, where you'll see real-time updates on its price, your unrealized gains or losses, and any dividends earned.

Buying your first stock is a significant step toward building your wealth, and you're now an active participant in the market.

Step 6: Monitor Your Investment

Owning a stock is just the beginning. Monitoring your investment is crucial to ensure your stock continues to align with your goals. This step involves tracking performance, staying informed about the company's developments, and making adjustments as necessary.

Track Your Stock's Performance

- **Portfolio Tracker:** Most brokers offer a portfolio tracker where you can view your stocks' current value, percentage gain or loss, and performance compared to benchmarks like the S&P 500. Regularly check this to gauge how your investment is doing.
- **Set Alerts:** Many brokerage platforms allow you to set price alerts, which notify you when your stock reaches a specific price. This feature helps you stay updated without constantly watching the market.

- **Revisit Your Research:** Continue reviewing the company's earnings reports, financial statements, and key metrics to ensure it's performing well. Metrics like revenue growth, profit margins, and debt levels provide insight into the company's ongoing health.

Stay Informed

- **News and Press Releases:** Major company news, such as product launches, earnings releases, and executive changes, can significantly impact stock prices. Set up news alerts for the companies you've invested in to stay on top of important updates.
- **Follow Market Trends:** Broader market trends, such as interest rate changes, geopolitical events, and economic reports, can also affect stock prices. Staying informed about the market environment helps you understand why your stock might be moving in a particular direction.

Make Informed Decisions

- **Hold, Buy More, or Sell:** Based on your stock's performance and your ongoing research, you'll need to decide whether to hold your position, buy more shares, or sell. Avoid making decisions based solely on short-term price movements; focus on your long-term strategy and the company's fundamentals.
- **Dividends and Reinvesting:** If your stock pays dividends, decide whether to take the cash or reinvest the dividends to buy more shares. Reinvesting dividends can accelerate your portfolio's growth through compounding.

By actively monitoring your investments, you can ensure they remain aligned with your goals and make adjustments as needed to optimize your portfolio.

Step 7: Have a Long-Term Mindset

Investing in stocks is not a get-rich-quick scheme. To succeed, it's important to adopt a long-term mindset, focusing on steady growth rather than chasing short-term gains. Here's how to maintain a long-term perspective:

Avoid Panic Selling

- **Embrace Market Volatility:** Stock prices fluctuate daily due to news, market sentiment, and other factors. Accept that volatility is a normal part of investing and doesn't necessarily reflect the company's long-term potential.
- **Stay Focused on Fundamentals:** Focus on the company's underlying fundamentals rather than short-term price movements. If the company continues to perform well and meet your investment thesis, there's usually no need to react to temporary market dips.

Think Long-Term

- **Compounding Returns:** The power of compounding means that the longer you hold a quality stock, the more you can benefit from its potential growth. This is why time in the market often beats trying to time the market.
- **Stick to Your Plan:** Define your investment goals, such as retirement, buying a home, or funding a child's

education, and align your stock purchases accordingly. Staying committed to your goals helps you navigate market ups and downs without losing sight of the bigger picture.

Review and Adjust Your Portfolio

- **Periodic Review:** Regularly review your portfolio to ensure it still meets your risk tolerance and financial objectives. Rebalance if necessary by adjusting your stock allocations or diversifying into other assets like bonds or real estate.
- **Continuous Learning:** Keep learning about investing by reading books, following market news, and studying successful investors' strategies. The more you understand, the better decisions you can make.

Maintaining a long-term perspective is key to achieving investing success. By staying disciplined and focused on your goals, you can weather the market's ups and downs and build a solid financial future.

Following these detailed steps will help you confidently buy your first stock and start your investing journey on the right foot. Remember, investing is a marathon, not a sprint—stay patient, keep learning, and stick to your plan for long-term success.

Chapter 14: How to Trade Momentum Stocks

Trading momentum stocks is a popular strategy that involves buying stocks that are showing strong upward or downward trends in price. Momentum trading aims to capitalize on the continuance of existing market trends, riding the wave of a stock's movement until signs indicate a potential reversal. This strategy can be highly profitable if executed correctly but also comes with significant risks, especially in volatile markets.

Here's a comprehensive guide on how to trade momentum stocks, covering the critical steps, strategies, and risk management techniques you need to know.

Step 1: Understand Momentum Trading

Before diving into trading momentum stocks, it's essential to grasp what momentum trading entails. Momentum trading is based on the idea that stocks that have performed well recently will continue to perform well, while stocks that have performed poorly will continue to decline. This approach is grounded in behavioral finance, where investor psychology often leads to sustained trends.

Key Principles of Momentum Trading:

- **Price Trends:** Momentum traders focus on stocks that are moving in a strong, defined direction, whether up or down. These trends are often driven by factors like earnings surprises, new product launches, or broader market sentiment.
- **Volume Confirmation:** High trading volume often accompanies momentum, confirming that there is strong investor interest in the stock. Volume spikes can indicate the start of a new momentum trend.

- **Speed and Timing:** Timing is crucial in momentum trading. The goal is to enter a position as the momentum builds and exit before it reverses. This requires quick decision-making and the ability to act on short-term price movements.

Momentum trading can be applied to both long (buying) and short (selling) positions, depending on the direction of the trend. The challenge is recognizing when a trend is likely to continue and when it might be losing steam.

Step 2: Find Momentum Stocks

Finding the right momentum stocks is critical to success. You'll need to identify stocks that are experiencing strong price movements and are likely to continue trending in the same direction. Here are some effective methods to find momentum stocks:

Screening for Momentum Stocks:

- **Use Stock Screeners:** Stock screeners are valuable tools for identifying momentum stocks. Set up screens to filter stocks based on criteria such as price changes, volume increases, relative strength, and moving average crossovers. Popular screeners include those available on platforms like Finviz, TradingView, and your brokerage's trading platform.
- **Relative Strength Index (RSI):** Use the RSI indicator to find stocks that are overbought or oversold. Momentum stocks often show high RSI values (above 70) during upward trends and low values (below 30) during downward trends.
- **52-Week Highs/Lows:** Stocks reaching new 52-week highs or lows are often exhibiting momentum. Stocks at new highs can indicate strong upward momentum, while those at new lows may be in a strong downward trend.
- **News and Earnings Reports:** Stocks with recent positive news, earnings surprises, or upgrades from analysts can experience

momentum. Keep an eye on earnings calendars, news feeds, and market-moving headlines.

Popular Momentum Indicators:

- **Moving Averages:** Simple moving averages (SMA) and exponential moving averages (EMA) are popular for identifying momentum. When a short-term moving average crosses above a long-term average (known as a golden cross), it signals upward momentum. The opposite (death cross) signals downward momentum.
- **MACD (Moving Average Convergence Divergence):** The MACD is a momentum indicator that shows the relationship between two moving averages of a stock's price. A crossover of the MACD line above the signal line indicates bullish momentum, while a crossover below indicates bearish momentum.
- **Average True Range (ATR):** ATR measures volatility and helps traders assess whether a stock's momentum is increasing. A rising ATR suggests growing volatility, which often accompanies strong momentum trends.

Finding momentum stocks requires ongoing research, and traders often adjust their screens to capture the stocks showing the strongest trends in real-time.

Step 3: Analyze the Stock Chart

Once you've identified potential momentum stocks, the next step is to analyze the stock charts to determine entry and exit points. Chart analysis helps you understand the stock's price action, volume, and potential support and resistance levels, guiding you to make informed trading decisions.

Key Chart Patterns for Momentum Trading:

- **Breakouts:** A breakout occurs when a stock price moves above a defined resistance level or below a support level, often accompanied by increased volume. Breakouts signal the start of a momentum move and provide entry points for traders.
- **Pullbacks:** In a strong uptrend, stocks often experience temporary declines or pullbacks before resuming their upward momentum. These pullbacks offer buying opportunities at lower prices.
- **Flags and Pennants:** These are short-term continuation patterns that indicate brief pauses in a strong trend before it continues. Flags are small rectangular patterns that slope against the prevailing trend, while pennants are small symmetrical triangles.

Using Technical Indicators:

- **Bollinger Bands:** These bands help identify the volatility of a stock. A breakout above the upper band can indicate strong upward momentum, while a breakout below the lower band can indicate strong downward momentum.
- **Volume Indicators:** On Balance Volume (OBV) and Volume Weighted Average Price (VWAP) are useful indicators. Rising OBV suggests that buying volume is driving the price higher, confirming upward momentum.
- **Candlestick Patterns:** Patterns like engulfing candles, dojis, and hammers can signal potential reversals or continuations of the trend, helping traders make entry and exit decisions.

Careful chart analysis allows traders to enter trades at optimal points and set realistic profit targets and stop-loss orders.

Step 4: Develop a Trading Plan

A well-defined trading plan is essential for trading momentum stocks successfully. Your plan should outline your entry and exit strategies, risk management techniques, and position sizing rules. A solid plan helps you stay disciplined and avoid making impulsive decisions.

Setting Entry Points:

- **Breakout Entry:** Entering on breakouts above resistance or below support is a common strategy. Look for strong volume to confirm the breakout.
- **Pullback Entry:** Wait for the stock to pull back to a support level, such as a moving average or previous breakout point, before entering. This allows you to buy at a lower price within the ongoing trend.

Defining Exit Strategies:

- **Profit Targets:** Set clear profit targets based on historical resistance levels, Fibonacci retracement levels, or technical indicators like the ATR. Knowing your exit point in advance helps lock in gains.
- **Trailing Stops:** Trailing stops move with the stock's price, locking in profits as the stock rises while limiting potential losses. This technique allows you to ride the trend until signs of a reversal appear.
- **Time-Based Exits:** In some cases, you may decide to exit a trade after a specific time frame, such as the end of the trading day or week, regardless of the price action. This can be useful in highly volatile environments.

Position Sizing:

- **Risk Management:** Determine how much of your portfolio you're willing to risk on each trade. A common rule is to risk no more than 1-2% of your trading capital on a single trade. This means setting stop-loss orders to exit a trade if it moves against you.

- **Scaling In and Out:** Consider scaling into positions by buying in increments rather than all at once. Similarly, scale out of positions gradually to lock in profits while staying in the trend.

A comprehensive trading plan keeps you focused, reduces emotional trading, and increases the likelihood of success.

Step 5: Execute the Trade

Once your plan is in place, it's time to execute the trade. Execution is not just about placing the order but also about managing the trade once it's live. Here's how to execute effectively:

Order Types for Momentum Trading:

- **Market Orders:** Use market orders for quick entry when you want to ensure execution, especially during strong momentum moves. However, be cautious of slippage in highly volatile stocks.
- **Limit Orders:** Limit orders allow you to specify the price at which you want to buy or sell, giving you control over the trade price. This is useful during pullbacks or when entering a breakout at a specific price level.
- **Stop Orders:** Use stop-loss orders to protect your capital. Place your stop below a recent support level for long trades or above resistance for short trades.

Managing the Trade:

- **Monitor Volume:** Keep an eye on volume to ensure the momentum is sustained. A sudden drop in volume could indicate weakening momentum and a potential reversal.
- **Adjust Stops:** Move your stop-loss to breakeven or above as the trade moves in your favor. This locks in gains and reduces risk as the trend progresses.
- **Be Ready to Exit:** Momentum stocks can reverse quickly, especially after sharp gains. Stay vigilant and be prepared to exit if

price action shows signs of weakening, such as a bearish candlestick pattern or a divergence in momentum indicators like the RSI or MACD.

Executing the trade according to your plan and staying disciplined is crucial to capturing the full potential of momentum moves.

Step 6: Manage Risk

Risk management is one of the most critical aspects of momentum trading. Because momentum stocks can be highly volatile, managing risk effectively helps protect your capital and ensures you can continue trading even after a few losing trades.

Set Stop-Loss Orders:

- **Initial Stop:** Place your initial stop-loss at a level that makes sense based on the chart, such as below a recent swing low or moving average. This limits your loss if the trade goes against you.
- **Trailing Stop:** As the trade moves in your favor, adjust your stop to lock in gains. Trailing stops move with the price, allowing you to capture more of the trend without exposing you to full downside risk.

Control Position Size:

- **Position Sizing Rules:** Determine your position size based on the amount of risk you're willing to take. Use a position sizing calculator or formula to ensure you're not overexposed on any single trade.
- **Avoid Over-Leveraging:** Leverage amplifies both gains and losses. Keep leverage within manageable levels, especially when trading highly volatile momentum stocks.

Diversify Your Trades:

- **Avoid Putting All Eggs in One Basket:** Diversify your trades across different stocks or sectors to reduce risk. Momentum trading one stock can be profitable, but spreading your trades can mitigate the impact of a loss.
- **Manage Correlations:** Be mindful of trading multiple stocks within the same sector, as they often move together. Diversifying across unrelated sectors can help balance your overall portfolio risk.

Effective risk management ensures that no single trade can significantly impact your trading capital, allowing you to stay in the game for the long term.

Step 7: Review and Learn from Each Trade

After each trade, take the time to review your performance and learn from the outcome. Momentum trading is a skill that improves with experience, and reflecting on both winning and losing trades helps refine your strategy.

Post-Trade Analysis:

- **Review Your Entry and Exit:** Did you enter at the optimal point? Were your exits timely? Analyze how well you followed your trading plan.
- **Evaluate Trade Management:** Assess how you managed the trade, including stop adjustments, scaling in or out, and adherence to your risk management rules.
- **Identify Mistakes:** Look for any mistakes, such as chasing a stock after a big move or setting stops too tight, and make note of how to avoid them in the future.

Keep a Trading Journal:

- **Log Every Trade:** Keep a detailed record of every trade, including the rationale, entry and exit points, stop-loss levels, and the result. This helps you track your progress and identify patterns in your trading behavior.
- **Learn Continuously:** Read books on momentum trading, follow market news, and study successful traders' strategies. The more knowledge you gain, the better equipped you'll be to adapt and improve.

Reviewing and learning from your trades builds your skills and helps you become a more disciplined and successful momentum trader.

Final Thoughts

Momentum trading can be an exciting and profitable strategy, but it requires a keen eye for spotting trends, disciplined execution, and robust risk management. By following these detailed steps and continuously honing your skills, you can effectively trade momentum stocks and potentially achieve consistent success in the market.

Here's a chart summarizing the key steps and concepts for trading momentum stocks:

Chart: How to Trade Momentum Stocks

Step	Description	Key Points
1. Understand Momentum Trading	Learn the fundamentals of momentum trading, which focuses on buying stocks with strong upward or downward trends.	- Price Trends - Volume Confirmation - Speed and Timing
2. Find Momentum Stocks	Identify stocks that are showing strong price movements and trends. Utilize tools and indicators for selection.	- Stock Screeners - RSI - 52-Week Highs/ Lows

Step	Description	Key Points
3. Analyze the Stock Chart	Examine stock charts to determine entry and exit points. Look for patterns and use technical indicators.	- News and Earnings - Breakouts - Pullbacks - Flags and Pennants - Bollinger Bands - Volume Indicators - Candlestick Patterns
4. Develop a Trading Plan	Create a plan outlining your entry and exit strategies, risk management, and position sizing.	- Entry Points - Exit Strategies - Position Sizing
5. Execute the Trade	Place your trade according to your plan and manage it as it unfolds.	- Market Orders - Limit Orders - Stop Orders - Managing the Trade
6. Manage Risk	Implement risk management strategies to protect your capital and minimize losses.	- Stop-Loss Orders - Position Sizing - Diversification
7. Review and Learn	Analyze your trades to learn from successes and mistakes. Keep a trading journal.	- Post-Trade Analysis - Trading Journal - Continuous Learning

This chart provides an overview of each step involved in trading momentum stocks, including essential concepts and strategies for successful trading.

Chapter 15: How to Generate Passive Income in the Stock Market

Generating passive income in the stock market involves investing in assets that provide regular income with minimal ongoing effort. Here are some effective strategies to achieve passive income through stock market investments:

1. Dividend Stocks

Overview: Dividend stocks are shares in companies that pay out a portion of their earnings to shareholders on a regular basis, typically quarterly. These dividends provide a steady stream of income.

How to Generate Passive Income:

- **Select Dividend-Paying Stocks:** Look for established companies with a history of paying and increasing dividends. Focus on those with a sustainable payout ratio and strong financial health.
- **Dividend Yield:** Calculate the dividend yield by dividing the annual dividend payment by the stock price. A higher yield indicates more income relative to the investment.
- **Dividend Reinvestment Plans (DRIPs):** Enroll in DRIPs to automatically reinvest dividends into additional shares, compounding your returns over time.

Pros and Cons:

- **Pros:** Regular income, potential for capital appreciation, and compounding through DRIPs.

- **Cons:** Dividend payments are not guaranteed and can be cut during economic downturns.

2. Real Estate Investment Trusts (REITs)

Overview: REITs are companies that own, operate, or finance income-producing real estate. They are required by law to distribute a significant portion of their income as dividends.

How to Generate Passive Income:

- **Invest in REITs:** Purchase shares of REITs that focus on various sectors like commercial, residential, or industrial properties.
- **Choose High-Yield REITs:** Look for REITs with high dividend yields, which indicate higher income potential.

Pros and Cons:

- **Pros:** Diversified exposure to real estate, regular income, and liquidity since REITs are traded on stock exchanges.
- **Cons:** REITs can be volatile and sensitive to interest rate changes.

3. Preferred Stocks

Overview: Preferred stocks are a type of equity security that provides fixed dividend payments and typically has priority over common stocks in dividend payments and liquidation.

How to Generate Passive Income:

- **Invest in Preferred Stocks:** Purchase shares of preferred stocks from reputable companies offering fixed dividends.
- **Evaluate Dividend Rates:** Compare the dividend rates and terms to select preferred stocks that offer attractive yields.

Pros and Cons:

- **Pros:** Fixed dividend payments and higher claim on assets than common stocks.
- **Cons:** Limited potential for capital appreciation and less voting rights compared to common stockholders.

4. Bonds and Bond Funds

Overview: Bonds are debt securities issued by governments or corporations that pay periodic interest payments. Bond funds pool money from multiple investors to invest in a diversified portfolio of bonds.

How to Generate Passive Income:

- **Invest in Individual Bonds:** Purchase bonds with favorable interest rates and credit ratings. Bonds pay regular interest (coupon payments) until maturity.
- **Invest in Bond Funds:** Buy shares of bond mutual funds or ETFs that provide diversified exposure to various bonds, generating regular income.

Pros and Cons:

- **Pros:** Regular interest payments and lower risk compared to stocks.
- **Cons:** Interest rate risk (bond prices fall when interest rates rise) and potential lower returns compared to stocks.

5. High-Yield Savings Accounts and Certificates of Deposit (CDs)

Overview: High-yield savings accounts and CDs offer higher interest rates compared to traditional savings accounts, providing a low-risk income stream.

How to Generate Passive Income:

- **Open High-Yield Savings Accounts:** Deposit funds into accounts offering higher interest rates, which pay regular interest on your balance.
- **Invest in CDs:** Purchase CDs with varying maturities to lock in higher interest rates and receive periodic interest payments.

Pros and Cons:

- **Pros:** Low risk and guaranteed returns up to FDIC insurance limits.
- **Cons:** Lower returns compared to stocks and limited liquidity with CDs (penalties for early withdrawal).

6. Peer-to-Peer (P2P) Lending

Overview: P2P lending platforms allow individuals to lend money directly to borrowers in exchange for interest payments.

How to Generate Passive Income:

- **Use P2P Lending Platforms:** Invest in loans on platforms like LendingClub or Prosper, where you earn interest as borrowers repay their loans.
- **Diversify Investments:** Spread your investment across multiple loans to reduce risk and enhance income potential.

Pros and Cons:

- **Pros:** Potential for higher returns compared to traditional savings accounts.
- **Cons:** Higher risk of borrower defaults and less liquidity.

7. Write Covered Calls

Overview: Writing covered calls involves selling call options on stocks you own, earning premiums from the options sold.

How to Generate Passive Income:

- **Own the Stock:** Hold shares of stocks you are willing to sell at a higher price.
- **Sell Call Options:** Write call options on those stocks, receiving premiums for the options. If the stock price exceeds the strike price, you may have to sell your shares.

Pros and Cons:

- **Pros:** Additional income from option premiums and potential for capital gains if the stock price rises.

- **Cons:** Limited upside potential (if the stock price rises significantly, you must sell at the strike price) and potential loss if the stock price falls.

8. Create and Sell Stock Market Courses or Content

Overview: If you have expertise in the stock market, creating and selling educational content can generate passive income.

How to Generate Passive Income:

- **Develop Courses:** Create online courses or e-books on stock market investing and sell them on platforms like Udemy or Teachable.
- **Monetize Content:** Use affiliate marketing or advertising to monetize a blog or YouTube channel focused on stock market education.

Pros and Cons:

- **Pros:** Potential for recurring income and leverage your expertise.
- **Cons:** Initial effort required to create content and ongoing marketing to attract buyers.

Final Thoughts

Generating passive income in the stock market requires strategic investments and a long-term perspective. By choosing the right assets, diversifying your investments, and focusing on income-generating opportunities, you can build a reliable stream of passive income while managing risk effectively.

Chapter 16:The One Thing You Should Never Do When Buying Value Stocks

When buying value stocks, one critical mistake to avoid is ***focusing solely on the stock's low price without considering the underlying business fundamentals****. This approach is often referred to as "value trap" investing, where investors are lured by seemingly cheap prices but end up with poor investments due to underlying issues with the company.*

Why This Is a Mistake:

1. **Ignoring Business Fundamentals:**
    - **Financial Health:** A low stock price might reflect deeper problems such as declining revenues, shrinking profit margins, or high levels of debt. Always analyze key financial metrics, including earnings reports, balance sheets, and cash flow statements, to assess the company's health.
    - **Competitive Position:** Consider the company's position within its industry. A stock might be undervalued because the company is losing market share, facing intense competition, or dealing with other structural issues.
2. **Not Understanding the Reason for the Low Price:**
    - **Temporary vs. Permanent Issues:** Determine whether the low price is due to temporary setbacks (e.g., a short-term problem that can be resolved) or permanent issues (e.g., fundamental shifts in the industry that could lead to long-term decline).
    - **Management and Strategy:** Evaluate the company's management team and strategic direction. Weak leadership or ineffective strategies can hinder long-term performance and recovery.

3. **Overlooking Growth Potential:**

    - **Future Prospects:** A low price does not necessarily mean the stock is a bargain if the company's future prospects are bleak. Assess growth opportunities, market trends, and the company's ability to adapt and innovate.

4. **Relying on Historical Valuations:**

    - **Past Performance:** While historical valuation metrics like price-to-earnings (P/E) ratios can provide insight, they should not be the sole factor in your decision. A low historical P/E might be justified by declining earnings or other negative trends.

5. **Neglecting Industry and Economic Conditions:**

    - **Broader Context:** The stock's performance can be influenced by broader economic conditions and industry-specific challenges. Ensure you understand the economic environment and industry dynamics that could impact the company's performance.

What to Do Instead:

1. **Conduct Thorough Research:**

    - **Fundamental Analysis:** Perform a comprehensive analysis of the company's financial statements, management quality, competitive position, and industry conditions.
    - **Valuation Metrics:** Use multiple valuation metrics (P/E ratio, price-to-book ratio, free cash flow) to get a complete picture of the stock's value.

2. **Understand the Company's Business Model:**

    - **Revenue and Profit Sources:** Know how the company makes money and whether its business model is sustainable.

- **Competitive Advantage:** Identify any competitive advantages or unique strengths that can contribute to long-term success.

3. **Assess Risk Factors:**

    - **Potential Risks:** Evaluate the risks associated with the company, including financial risks, market risks, and operational risks.
    - **Management and Strategy:** Consider the effectiveness of the company's management and their strategic plans for addressing challenges and seizing opportunities.

4. **Diversify Your Investments:**

    - **Avoid Concentration:** Diversify your portfolio to mitigate the impact of any single investment's poor performance. Avoid putting too much capital into one stock, regardless of how undervalued it appears.

5. **Monitor and Reevaluate:**

    - **Ongoing Assessment:** Regularly review the performance of your investments and stay updated on any changes in the company's fundamentals or industry conditions.

By avoiding the trap of focusing solely on a stock's low price and instead thoroughly analyzing the company's fundamentals, you can make more informed decisions and increase your chances of successful value investing.

Here's a chart summarizing the key points on what to avoid and what to focus on when buying value stocks:

Chart: Key Considerations When Buying Value Stocks

Aspect	What to Avoid	What to Focus On
Stock Price	Focusing solely on the low stock price without understanding why it's	Consider the reasons behind the low price and the company's fundamentals.

Aspect	What to Avoid	What to Focus On
	low.	
Business Fundamentals	Ignoring the company's financial health, competitive position, and management quality.	Analyze financial statements, competitive position, and management effectiveness.
Reason for Low Price	Assuming the low price is a bargain without understanding the underlying issues.	Determine if the low price is due to temporary issues or fundamental problems.
Growth Potential	Overlooking future growth prospects and relying solely on past performance.	Evaluate future growth opportunities, market trends, and innovation potential.
Valuation Metrics	Relying only on historical valuation metrics like P/E ratio without context.	Use a range of valuation metrics and compare them to industry norms and company prospects.
Industry and Economic Context	Neglecting the impact of broader economic and industry conditions on the company.	Assess the economic environment and industry trends that could affect the company's performance.
Risk Factors	Ignoring potential risks and challenges facing the company.	Evaluate financial, market, and operational risks, and the company's strategies for managing them.
Diversification	Concentrating too much capital in a single undervalued stock.	Diversify investments to reduce risk and avoid overexposure to any single stock.
Ongoing Monitoring	Making a one-time investment decision without follow-up.	Regularly review and reassess the investment, keeping up-to-date with company performance and industry conditions.

This chart provides a clear overview of what to avoid and what to focus on when buying value stocks, helping you make more informed and effective investment decisions.

FAQ

1. How does selling shares on the stock exchange benefit companies?

Selling shares on the stock exchange allows companies to raise capital by issuing stock to investors. This capital can be used for expansion, research and development, debt reduction, or other corporate needs. It also increases the company's visibility and credibility in the market.

2. What time does the New York Stock Exchange open?

The New York Stock Exchange (NYSE) opens at 9:30 AM Eastern Time (ET) on regular trading days.

3. What time does the New York Stock Exchange close?

The NYSE closes at 4:00 PM Eastern Time (ET) on regular trading days.

4. Which stock market exchange is recognized as the oldest in the world?

The Amsterdam Stock Exchange, established in 1602, is recognized as the oldest stock market exchange in the world.

5. What type of investments were first traded at the New York Stock Exchange?

The NYSE initially traded bonds and shares of the Dutch East India Company, which was the first company to issue stock.

6. How does a company benefit by having their stock listed on an exchange?
Listing on an exchange provides a company with access to a larger pool of investors, increases its market visibility, enhances its credibility, and often results in a more liquid market for its shares. It also allows the company to raise capital through public stock offerings.

7. What is a stock exchange Everfi?
Everfi is an educational platform that provides interactive learning resources on financial literacy, including information about stock exchanges and other financial concepts.

8. What is a reason the New York Stock Exchange began to trade mostly stocks?
The NYSE began to trade mostly stocks due to the increasing popularity of equity investments and the demand from companies seeking to raise capital through stock issuance.

9. What is the primary purpose of a stock exchange?
The primary purpose of a stock exchange is to provide a regulated and transparent platform for buying and selling securities, such as stocks and bonds, facilitating capital formation and liquidity for investors.

10. As an investor, what is the risk involved in investing in companies on the stock exchange?
Investing in companies on the stock exchange involves risks such as market volatility, economic fluctuations, company-

specific issues, and the potential for loss of capital. Investors should be aware of these risks and consider their investment goals and risk tolerance.

11. What are exchange-traded funds (ETFs)?

Exchange-traded funds (ETFs) are investment funds that trade on stock exchanges, similar to individual stocks. They hold a diversified portfolio of assets, such as stocks, bonds, or commodities, and aim to track the performance of a specific index or sector.

12. What is an ETF example?

An example of an ETF is the SPDR S&P 500 ETF (SPY), which aims to track the performance of the S&P 500 Index.

13. What is ETF and how does it work?

An ETF is a fund that trades on an exchange and holds a collection of assets, such as stocks or bonds. It works by pooling investors' money to invest in these assets, and its shares are bought and sold on the stock exchange throughout the trading day.

14. Are ETFs halal?

The halal status of ETFs depends on their underlying assets and structure. ETFs that invest in businesses or assets that comply with Islamic finance principles are considered halal. It's important to check the specific ETF's compliance with Shariah laws.

15. Is an ETF better than a stock?

Whether an ETF is better than a stock depends on an investor's goals. ETFs offer diversification and lower risk compared to individual stocks, but stocks can offer higher potential returns. The choice depends on the investor's risk tolerance and investment strategy.

16. Is ETF a Cryptocurrency?

No, an ETF is not a cryptocurrency. An ETF is a type of investment fund, while cryptocurrencies are digital or virtual currencies.

17. Is ETF a debt or equity?

ETFs can hold both debt (bonds) and equity (stocks) depending on their investment strategy. The underlying assets of the ETF determine whether it focuses on debt, equity, or a mix of both.

18. Are ETFs legal?

Yes, ETFs are legal investment vehicles and are regulated by financial authorities in various countries.

19. Is ETF a good investment?

ETFs can be a good investment for many people due to their diversification, liquidity, and relatively low cost. However, the suitability of an ETF depends on an individual's investment goals and risk tolerance.

20. Do ETFs make money?

ETFs can make money through price appreciation, dividends from underlying assets, and interest income. The return depends on the performance of the assets held in the ETF.

21. Are ETFs good for beginners?

Yes, ETFs can be good for beginners because they offer

diversification and are typically easier to understand and manage compared to individual stocks.

22. Is it better to buy bitcoin or ETF?
The decision between buying bitcoin or an ETF depends on your investment goals and risk tolerance. Bitcoin is highly volatile and speculative, while ETFs provide diversification and are generally considered less risky.

23. How to buy an ETF?
To buy an ETF, you need to open a brokerage account, research and select the ETF you wish to invest in, and place an order through your brokerage account.

24. Is ETF a currency?
No, an ETF is not a currency. It is a type of investment fund that holds various assets.

25. What is the best ETF to buy?
The best ETF to buy depends on your investment goals, risk tolerance, and market outlook. Popular ETFs include those that track major indices like the S&P 500 or specific sectors such as technology.

26. Does ETF pay dividends?
Many ETFs pay dividends if the underlying assets generate income. The amount and frequency of dividends depend on the ETF's holdings.

27. What are the disadvantages of ETFs?
Disadvantages of ETFs include management fees, potential tracking error, and the risk of market fluctuations. Additionally,

some ETFs may have lower liquidity, which can impact trading costs.

28. Can an ETF become zero?
While it's unlikely, an ETF can potentially become worthless if the assets it holds lose all their value. This is more likely in highly volatile or niche markets.

29. Can I withdraw ETFs anytime?
You can sell your ETF shares anytime during market hours, but the ability to "withdraw" cash from your ETF investment depends on selling the shares on the market.

30. Why are my ETFs losing money?
ETFs may lose money due to market declines, poor performance of the underlying assets, or other economic factors. It’s important to review the ETF's performance and market conditions.

31. How to make money on ETF?
You can make money on an ETF through capital appreciation (selling the ETF for more than you paid) and receiving dividends if the ETF holds income-generating assets.

32. How much money should I put in an ETF?
The amount to invest in an ETF should align with your investment goals, risk tolerance, and overall portfolio strategy. Diversification and proper asset allocation are key considerations.

33. How long do you hold ETFs?
The holding period for ETFs depends on your investment

strategy. Some investors hold ETFs long-term for growth, while others may trade them more frequently based on market conditions.

34. Are ETF funds risky?
ETFs carry risk, which varies based on the assets they hold. Risk levels depend on the underlying investments and market conditions. Diversification typically reduces risk compared to individual stocks.

35. When to buy ETFs?
The timing for buying ETFs should be based on your investment goals, market conditions, and analysis of the ETF's performance. It's important to consider your overall investment strategy.

36. How many shares of ETF should I buy?
The number of ETF shares to buy depends on your investment amount, risk tolerance, and portfolio diversification needs. It's important to assess how the ETF fits into your overall investment strategy.

37. Who owns an ETF?
ETFs are owned by the investors who purchase shares of the fund. The fund is managed by a financial institution or asset manager.

38. Why I don't invest in ETFs?
Reasons for not investing in ETFs could include concerns about fees, lack of understanding, preference for individual stocks, or specific investment goals that ETFs do not meet.

39. Can I take my ETF money?

You can sell ETF shares to access your investment money, subject to market conditions and any potential trading fees.

40. Which ETF is best for beginners?

For beginners, ETFs that track major indices like the S&P 500 (e.g., SPDR S&P 500 ETF) or broad market ETFs are often recommended due to their diversification and lower risk.

41. What is the top 3 ETF?

The top ETFs can vary based on criteria such as performance, assets under management, or popularity. Examples include the SPDR S&P 500 ETF (SPY), the Invesco QQQ Trust (QQQ), and the iShares MSCI Emerging Markets ETF (EEM).

42. What is better than ETF?

Whether something is better than an ETF depends on individual investment goals. Some might prefer individual stocks, mutual funds, or other investment vehicles based on their specific needs.

43. Does ETF expire?

ETFs do not expire. They remain on the market as long as the fund provider continues to manage them and there is investor interest.

44. Do ETFs go to zero?

While rare, ETFs can potentially become worthless if the underlying assets lose all their value. However, this is unlikely

Tableof Content

www.ingramcontent.com/pod-product-compliance
Lightning Source LLC
LaVergne TN
LVHW051102210926
848486LV00019B/403